3898·PT 78

LOOK & SEE

LOOK & SEE
ANTHONY BURRILL

 Thames & Hudson

287-5

A.B.

2604

FOREWORD
ERIK KESSELS

Anthony Burrill and I have worked together on several collaborative projects over the years; what started as a professional relationship has grown into a genuine friendship based on our mutual obsession and appreciation for design and communication.

Burrill has good taste in typography, always has had. His typographic palate is not content with the mainstream or popular type that you'll find in typographic annuals and sourcebooks. Burrill's tastes are more exotic, and he gets his fix out in the real world: a piece of old advertising on a wall somewhere, the freehand scrawl of a graffiti artist, or typographic treasures hidden in unexpected places.

Burrill likes his inspiration to go. Some people can hold their inspiration in their heads but others, like Anthony, surround themselves with inspiration, with pieces of type and snippets of conversations that feed both his work and his creative process on a daily basis.

I often talk about people's metaphorical backyards; the places where they plant their inspiration and grow their ideas before they present them in their front garden (as the finished product) for everyone to see. Anthony Burrill's backyard is more like a small country; a magical place full of eclectic printed ephemera, typographical games, strange photographs and an extensive collection of vernacular printing examples. The strongest creative minds I've met over the years are usually the ones who spend plenty of time rummaging around in their backyard experimenting, deconstructing, reconstructing and just enjoying all of the weird and wonderful things that you can derive inspiration from.

This book is a rare invitation to take a guided tour around Anthony Burrill's extensive collection of pieces that inspire and drive his work. See this as an inspirational guide to metaphorical landscape gardening – it's time to get your hands dirty...

INTRODUCTION
ANTHONY BURRILL

Where does your inspiration come from? It's a question I'm asked regularly, and a difficult one to answer quickly. One answer is to look at the things I collect and keep, the odd scraps that I've picked up and valued enough to hang on to.

At art college we were encouraged to keep sketchbooks. This was a new idea to me, and everybody spent a lot of time perfecting the look of these visual diaries. Looking through other people's sketchbooks always gave a better insight to their creative personality than their finished pieces of work. Here you could see the development of a creative mind and where the information and inspiration were coming from.

My sketchbooks became a place where I kept the everyday ephemera that I picked up along the way. I looked for anything that tickled my fancy, an odd arrangement of type, a strange image or a curious use of language. This was the stuff that connected with me and fuelled my development as a designer.

ANTHONY BURRILL

It's vital to examine the world around us and understand how we interact with visual communication. Seeing things for what they really are, and how they sometimes unintentionally reveal a bigger truth.

I continue to collect this material; my appetite only increases with time. I felt I was collecting it for a reason, hoping that it would form a collection that would be of interest and worth sharing.

So here it is: all the interesting things I've found, and the stories attached to them.

JUNK CAR

WE BU

23-9-21-5-12

23-9-21-5-12

SE

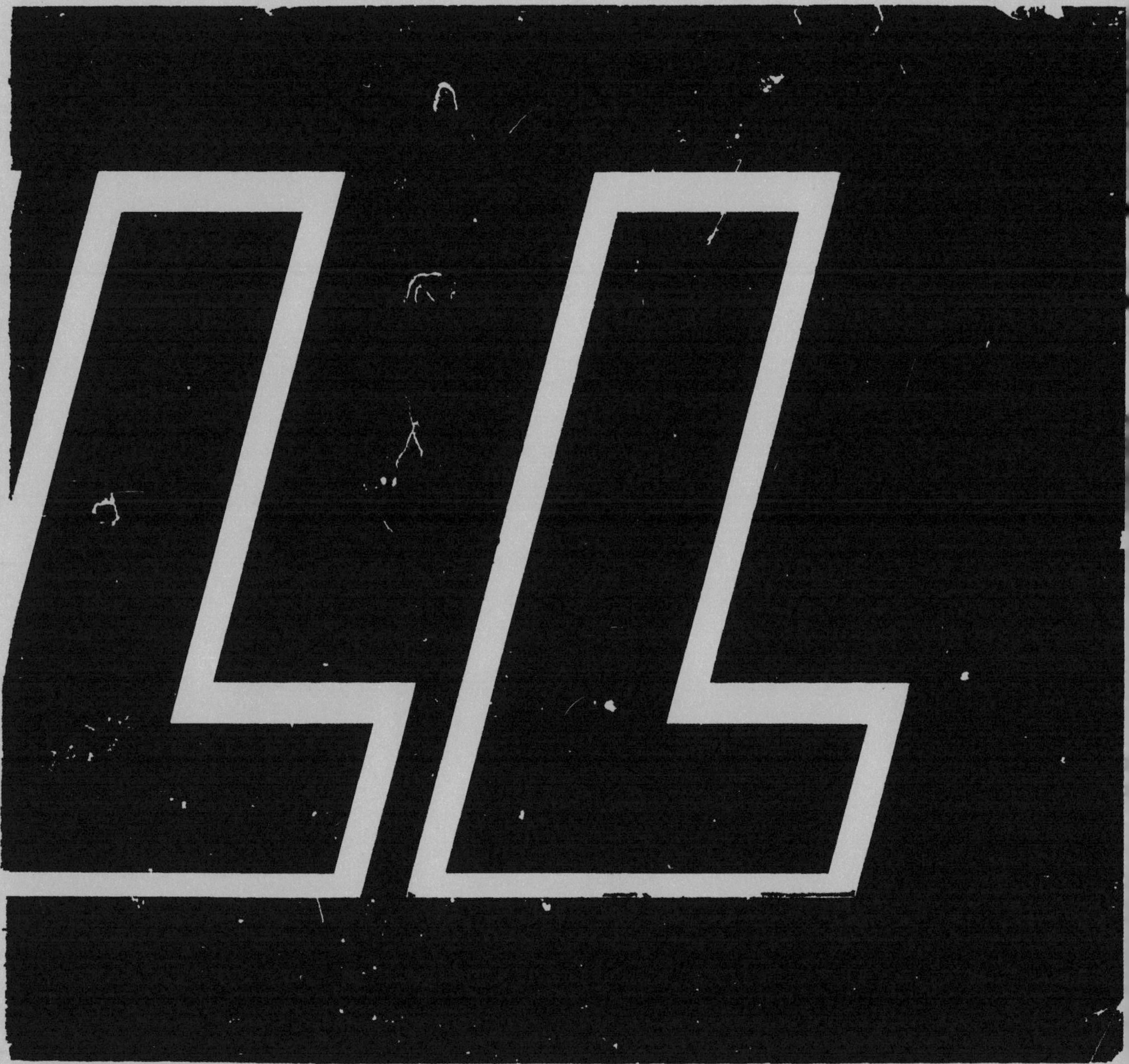

Next time you find yourself somewhere new, take the time to really examine your surroundings, step away from the crowds of people and take in the unfamiliar streets.

The smallest things can often be the most revealing, so make sure to seek out all of the overlooked corners and neglected, forgotten places for inspiration.

Collecting visual inspiration feeds creativity, so always encourage yourself to look differently at the world. For example, if you notice that everyone is walking one way, then find a different route, take the long way around, and there's a good chance you'll spot something interesting.

My keen eye spotted this
set of instructions inside
a packet of sticking
plasters, shortly after
badly cutting my finger
with a scalpel blade. I like
the beautiful simplicity
of this diagram, which
when enlarged resembles
a Pop Art painting by
Roy Lichtenstein.

Step-by-step guides
like this remind me of a
film storyboard – a short
illustrated sequence that
breaks down action into
several sequential frames.
I can picture this series
of drawings translated
into moving images; a
looping film of repetitive
kinetic energy, continually
wrapping and unwrapping
an injured digit.

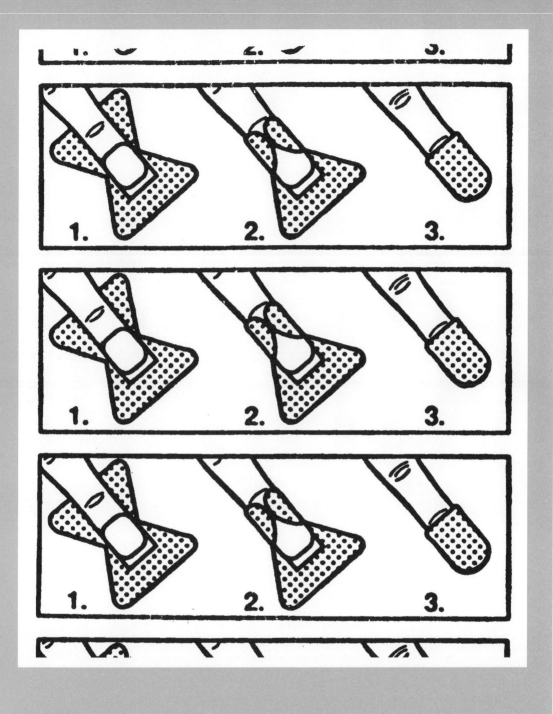

20819

WINDSHIELD STUB—RECEIPT
NOT A CLAIM CHECK

Lic. # _____

I picked up this windshield stub on my first trip to New York in the early 1990s. I think the tickets were something to do with valet parking; an alien concept to somebody who grew up in England. This ticket and many hundreds like it littered every sidewalk in Manhattan. I collected so many that by the end of the trip I stopped picking them up, satisfied that I had more than enough examples to fill my sketchbook.

I love the condensed letterform of the numbers; they're geometric and elegant. Modern, but with an echo of the past, just like the city itself. I was surprised by how European New York felt to me. The sense of history was everywhere, something I wasn't expecting.

When I'm exploring an unfamiliar city I look down as well as up, scanning the pavement for scraps of paper that act as grubby souvenirs of the trip. Each new place has its own distinct visual language. From bus tickets to laundry receipts, these are the physical reminders that I take home with me.

They capture something that photographs can't, a physicality of time and place that connects a tactile sensation with a real place. A reminder of how I felt in a particular location on a specific day.

The first car I drove was a Ford Fiesta. It was pale blue and looked like a three-dimensional drawing of a car, boxy in its styling and satisfyingly boring to look at. It was never going to win any beauty competitions, but I loved its anonymity and average performance. When I found these clip-art drawings of cars, they reminded me of that first car. They're from the early 1980s and share a similar everyday aesthetic that has now become unwittingly fashionable.

The graphic language of road signs has a particular appeal for me. They're a reminder of the world as a visual place full of systems and information told through graphic communication. Roads are like gigantic diagrams, with their dotted lines and hatched margins, telling us where to go and when to move. I'm inspired by the abstract nature of the highway landscape, its merges and junctions delineated with graphic flourishes.

Zig-zag markings outside schools, zebra crossings and double yellow lines, rigorously designed for function and road safety. These graphic demarcations are vast visual compositions. Their high-contrast colours of black, white and yellow are vibrant and eye-catching. When viewed close up, give-way signs and crooked directional arrows become hard-edged abstractions. I even like the way the pure graphic design applied to freshly laid tarmac gradually becomes distressed by age and wear.

Look down and look up!

ANTHONY BURRILL

(10pt) 0.098 inch 2,5 mm

A A A A A A A A A A A A A A A A A **11**

A A A A A A A A A A A A A A A A A B

B B B B B B B B B B B B B B B B B B

B B B Ç Ç Ç Ç Ç Ç Ç Ç Ç C C C C C C

C C C C C C C D D D D D D D D D D D

D D D D D D D D D D D D E E E E E

E E E E E E E E E E E E E E E E E E

E E E E E E E E E E E E E E E E E E

E E E F F F F F F F F F F F F F F F F

F G G G G G G G G G G G G G G G G

G G G G G H H H H H H H H H H H H

H H H H H H H H H I I I I I I I I I I I

I I I I I I I I I I I I I I I J J J J J J J

J J J J J J J J K K K K K K K K K K K

K K K K K K K K K K L L L L L L L L L

L L L L L L L L L L L L L L L L L M M

M M M M M M M M M M M M M M M M

M M M N N N N N N N N N N N N N N

N N N N N N N N N N N N N N N N N N

N N O O O O O O O O O O O O O O O

O O O O O O O O O O O P P P P P P

P P P P P P P P P P P P P P P Q Q Q

Q Q Q Q Q R R R R R R R R R R R R

R R R R R R R R R R R R R R R S S S

S S S S S S S S S S S S S S S S S S

S S S S S S S S T T T T T T T T T T

T T T T T T T T T T T T T T T T T T

T U U U U U U U U U U U U U U U U U

U U U U U U U U V V V V V V V V V V V

V V V V V V W W W W W W W W X X X X X

X X X Y Y Y Y Y Y Y Y Z Z Z Z Z Z Z Z

Æ Æ Ø Ø & & ? ? ? ! ! ! ;;;;;;;;;;; :: ≈≈≈ "" : ((∘))

A sea of repeating 10-point letters that resembles an avant-garde typographic poem read out loud. AAAAAAAAAAAAAAAAAAAAAAAAAA!

I found this sheet of tiny rub-down letters in a stationery shop in Berlin. A mundane example of high street graphic ephemera that, when viewed differently, transforms itself into something unfamiliar.

New ideas are made by taking ordinary objects and applying creative thinking. Taking the everyday for a walk to an interesting new place. Isolating the familiar through the lens of poetry to reveal a new story based on truth but inspired by imagination.

Inspiration is all around – you just have to know where to look. An idea for a poem can be found in a scrap of paper on the pavement. You have to train yourself to see things from a new angle.

This is how I think. How can something that appears familiar be transformed into something new and inspiring?

I'm inspired by the functionality of this arrangement of letters. A regular grid of abstract symbols that when grouped together correctly spells out words. Look at them again, these miniature abstract symbols that enable us to communicate the most profound ideas and thoughts.

All of this for a few euros on the way to catch a train.

These letterpress printed bookmaker's cards were found by my friend Tim at the greyhound racing track in Catford, South London.

The design of each card follows a similar layout: a series of large decorative numerals and the details of the individual bookmaker are printed boldly in black with blocks of colour in the background completing the design.

The large numerals are particularly interesting to me, with the number spelt out in words within each character. A double emphasis that helps clear up any confusion, and no room for interpretation.

The letterforms are originally Victorian in design, elaborate and beautifully crafted. The bold simplicity of the layout and the repetition of the distinctive numerals act as a foil to the individual character of the letterforms.

Tim collected these cards over twenty years ago. I imagine the modern-day counterparts lack the beauty of these historic examples. They might not even exist any longer, with their function rendered useless.

An example of a lost design that was once part of the everyday graphic landscape, and which has sadly disappeared from daily use.

ANTHONY BURRILL

DICKINS

Portsea London E9

TWO

S S S

2

TWO

THREE

MORRY PETER

FOUR 4 5 FIVE 7 SEVEN

FOUR 4 5 FIVE 5 7 SEVEN

N N

SEVEN 7 5 FIVE FOUR 7

SEVEN 7 5 FIVE FOUR 7

FIVE 5

MORRY PETER

RRROO
ETERSØ
78TY RRAPA
1HNC
23678 2
4571872
485764

GOT MOVERS?

2 MEN/Truck

$65 Per Hour

818
287-5260

AEIO
YUAE
IOU.

HE

my n

HE

my n

LO

me is

LO

me is

Arrows are my favourite graphic devices; they are hard to ignore. They point up, down, left and right all at the same time. Not only do they provide an aid to direction but they create a visual tension that feels like movement. A direction of focus, leading the eye of the viewer to its intended target. A word or phrase can be emphasized by the use of an arrow; a visual explosion that, when detonated, creates a huge effect that can't be ignored.

What is it?

Where is it?

It's over here!

When grouped together like this, the arrows provide a sense of movement that draws us in. We can't help but look at where the arrows are pointing.

What are they pointing at?

What am I looking at?

When were we all taught that an arrow depicts a direction of travel or focus of attention?

The graphic arrow is a visual echo of a pointing finger.

It's over there, just there!

Can you see it?

ANTHONY BURRILL

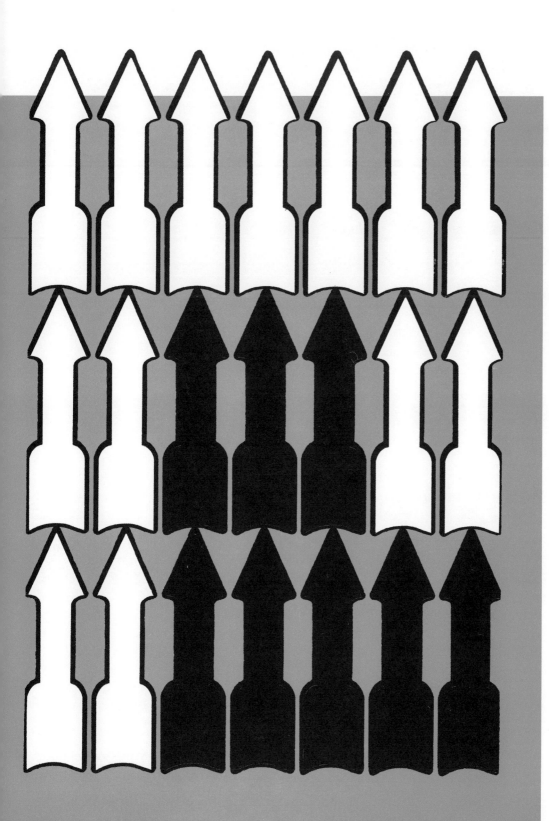

№ _____   **49**

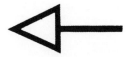

The combination of decorative border and a rubber-stamped number make this found inspection slip an essay in graphic information. The formality of the layout, with space allocated for the addition of a number, is rendered redundant by the ad-hoc placement of the numerals.

There is no practical reason for the serpentine border, and no need for the line marked 'No'. Number 49 could easily have been stamped on to a blank piece of paper, and we would have had all the information we needed.

Graphic flourishes like this are echoes of an outdated visual language that has its roots firmly in the Victorian era with all its decorative indulgences. Something that was swept away by the austere rationalism of graphic modernism.

This design feels nostalgic and dated to our modern eyes. Archaeological evidence of a former language, which is now long forgotten; that has somehow time-travelled into the present day as a reminder of how things used to be.

LOOK & SEE

I carefully removed this beautiful
letterpress poster from a notice board
in rural France on 19 September 1994. I
can be so sure of the location and date
because of the information printed on
the poster. I felt justified taking it off
the wall, as the advertised event had
taken place. It didn't feel like stealing,
as the intended use of the poster had
passed. It was no longer needed, and I
felt it was much better that, rather than
being disposed of, the poster would
be added to my growing collection of
printed ephemera.

Looking back, I wish I'd found out
where the poster had originally been
printed. The range of typefaces used is
wonderful, and hints at a collection of
wood type that must have been vast and
varied. Maybe the printer still exists,
in the same way that my local printer
Adams of Rye still survives. However, I
fear the French printer may now have
been replaced by the ubiquity of the
desktop computer and the bland fate of
system typefaces.

ANTHONY BURRILL

GEMOZAC

MIGNOT - JONZAC - R.M. 386 77 17

18 Dimanche SEPTEMBRE 94

à 15 heures

THÉ
- Dansant -

animé par l'orchestre

Jim PETER

Pâtisserie Kemia - Roses

organisé par

Chantal et Sandrine

Réservations : 46 90 72 64 - 46 90 74 06

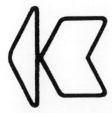

Another example of an instructional guide, this time to correct photographic exposures. It is set in a strangely claustrophobic interior lit by a single lamp, which casts an ominous pool of light across the room, creating an unsettling atmosphere.

The lighting conditions provide a challenge for the silhouetted photographer standing behind his tripod. The subject of his photographic efforts is the strange conjoined couple, whose shapes have overlapped and morphed into a bizarre two-headed creature.

As you can tell, my imagination has been sparked by this thought-provoking scene. All this from an innocent guide to taking better indoor family snaps that I found inside a packet of 35mm film.

I've included this mirth-inducing paper bag design not only for its humour, but for its sheer graphic exuberance. The wonderful combination of eye-catching illustration and fulsome typography underline this gem of pure comedy translated into visual communication. It looks like a saucy TV sitcom from the 1970s has been co-opted into visual form. A not-so-subtle joke to advertise a 24-hour convenience store in the famous Dutch city.

I was in Amsterdam working with Erik Kessels on a campaign for my favourite client, the Hans Brinker Hostel, when I chanced upon this graphic gem. I couldn't resist exploring the shop to see what delights were on sale. The reality, however, was to prove less than exciting. The Big Banana shop actually sold daily food items, fresh fruit and magazines. I'd have to look elsewhere for something a little more exciting.

ANTHONY BURRILL

Big Bananas

AMSTERDAM   night shop

The mechanics of printed reproduction create interesting and unexpected by-products. For example, these marks are designed as an aid for printers to measure ink levels and the amount of spread produced during the printing process. But when viewed differently – in this case, in extreme magnification – they become beautiful works of art.

The precise graphic information is rendered in loose inky shapes, bleeding and merging across the surface of the paper. The tension between precision and the organic nature of ink is what makes this example so interesting. The way boxes of varying densities of dot pattern fill up and darken feels like the equivalent of a piece of music to me. I can almost hear the swelling of the music as it grows and multiplies within the restrictions of the geometric space. The starburst shape and concentric polygons mirror audio explosions of sound, and when viewed as a repeat it could represent a building rhythm or melody.

Looking at abstract images conjures ideas of musical composition and abstraction in music, a correspondence that I can visualize. I suppose image patterns and sounds live together in the same part of my brain, which is why I find it so satisfying when they're combined.

ANTHONY BURRILL

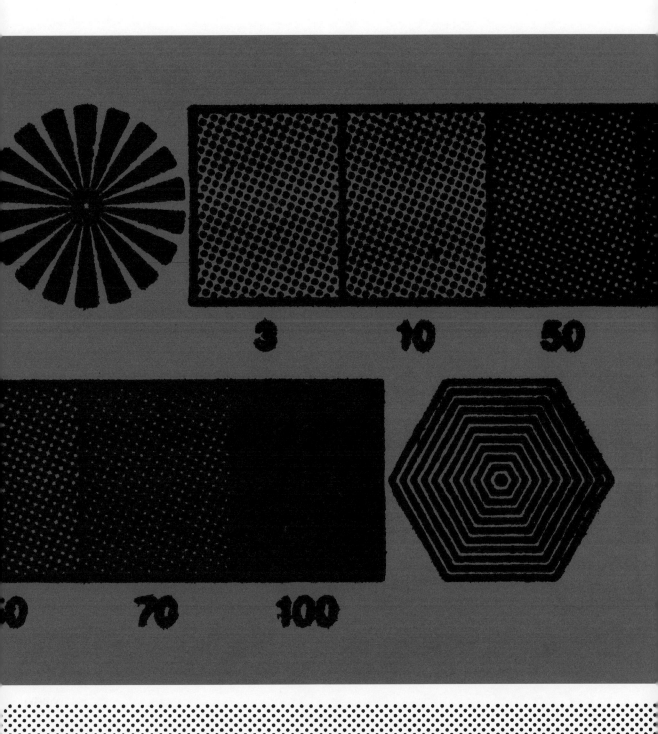

3　10　50

50　70　100

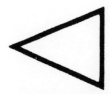

Dollar signs are arranged on a grid to create numerals found on packing wrapped around a stack of newspapers outside a newsagent's shop in South London. Maybe the dollar symbol was chosen for its print density in order to make the numbers appear more legible. Or maybe it was picked in reference to the world of commerce.

Using repeat symbols to create letterforms is a hangover from the early dot-matrix printer technology. The machines of the time were unable to print large areas of dense tone, so their rudimentary system was based on the typewriter with its approach to committing ink to paper.

The click and whirr of the dot-matrix printer as it goes about its work is now a far-off audio memory, long superseded by the automaton-like 'woos' of a laser printer. What we've gained in clarity and saturation, we've lost in the exciting physicality of ink being literally punched into paper.

This found scrap gave me an idea for a family of typefaces, with each character set out in a grid of tiny repeated letters. It's still on my 'to do' list, an ever-growing series of things to try out and projects to realize.

Inspiration for new work comes in unexpected places like this. Always be aware, and have your idea-finding radar switched on at all times.

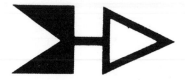

All available space has been filled on this sheet of self-adhesive letters. Even the smallest gaps have been populated by additional asterisk and punctuation symbols. This beautiful jumble of letters has a lively appearance. The letters and numbers are arranged in columns and lines, but these have been disrupted to provide more capacity.

Numbers, letters and punctuation marks jostle for position on the page, but never spill over or overlap. It's an ordered chaos. The letterforms are in themselves quite simple, but possess just enough character to look interesting. Some letters are upside down to make better use of the space, and this adds further to the sense of anarchic freedom.

When viewed in isolation, this purely functional arrangement takes on the appearance of a piece of cutting-edge graphic design. It could be mistaken for the latest piece of work by a hot design studio for a cool new brand. But it isn't, it's a humble set of stick-on letters that I found in a stationery shop in Brazil.

ANTHONY BURRILL

AAAABC RUN!UN

BCDDEJ VAXXY

EEEFFG TIRNY

GK {≡} !WM44

HJH 112233

KL7 MM **5566!

PP &OO **897700

",",Q*SS 89¿?*&

QNNOO

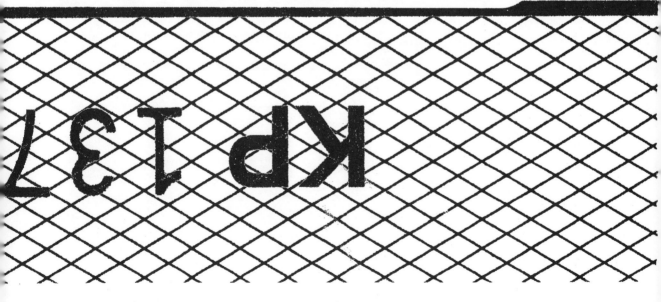

This is a piece of agricultural graphic ephemera 'found' on a holiday in France. It was quite irresponsible of me to 'acquire' this piece of signage, but it was hard to resist. It's sometimes necessary to bend the rules, and in this case it was vitally important that this wonderful example of typography could help inspire me at home.

In English, 'clôture électrique' means electric fence. I didn't need to translate the text, though; I knew by its proximity to the charged barrier that this sign was important, both for its safety message and its unique approach to type design.

Look closely at the curve of the letter R, and see how it contrasts with the other usually curved letterforms, the C, O, U and Q. Those letters have been given chunky right angles, while the R is left in its more recognizable state. Why is that? Why did the sign designer choose to leave the R with a curve? That's what drew my interest to this particular sign and why I had to have it, even if it meant flouting safety laws.

The addition of the lightning strikes and the Gallic brand name displayed in a curvaceous ribbon only add to the overall oddness and jarring typographic juxtaposition of this wonderful little sign.

Is it possible to have something special that is even more special than another special thing?

A special special special?

It's an odd choice of word to display in an elaborate graphic crest. Special isn't the first superlative on the list; it's quite mild. You'd think of something being wonderful or marvellous. But calling something special is almost on a par with it being 'quite good'.

But this fragment of packaging is special, at least to me. I found it stuck to a bag of dried bananas when I was travelling around India in the 1990s. This trip was inspiring in many ways, not least for the amount of graphic inspiration I gained during the trip. I collected lots of examples of packaging and printed material; all of it using language in an interesting and novel way.

Businesses were described as **TOP QUALITY**, taxis had **MODERN** written on the bodywork. Seemingly random word associations made unlikely poetry part of the everyday experience.

So this bag of dried bananas became quite special to me, different from all the other bags of fruit on display in the market.

ANTHONY BURRILL

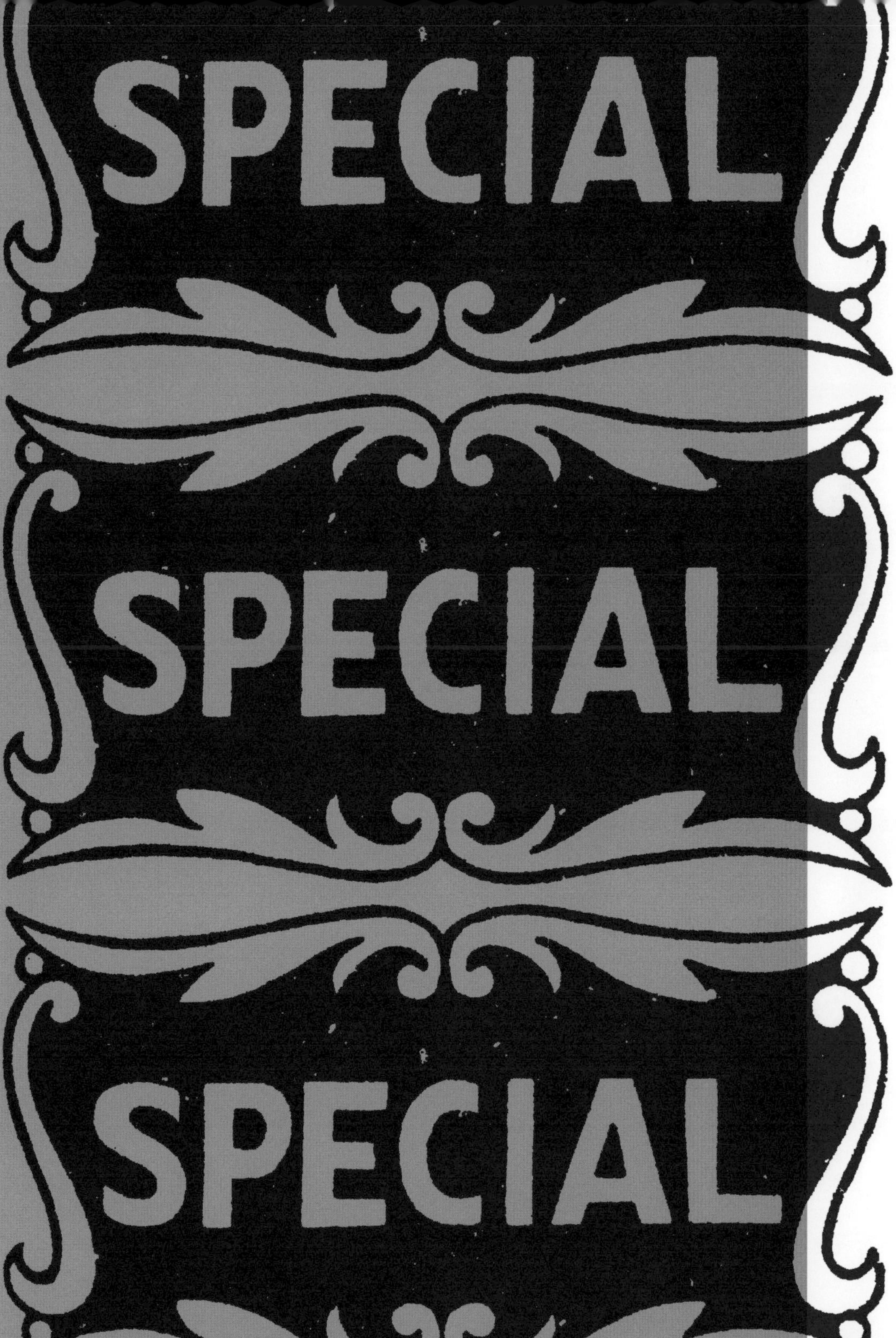
SPECIAL
SPECIAL
SPECIAL

QRST
UVWX
YZ
▶&

1 2 3 4
5 6 7 8
9 0 —

KLM
NOP!
QRS

Fill up your sketchbook with the visual evidence of daily life, keep hold of absolutely everything, file it carefully away, and it will provide you with a rich source of reference in the future.

Make rough collages of the things that you gather, and add in notes and quick sketches.

This found material is your creative playground; it's a space for exploration and experiment. Combining these found elements with your own personal notes adds further layers of meaning to the material.

I came across this press clipping, taken from a local newspaper, when I lived in South London in the 1990s. While browsing the small ads section, it struck me as odd and amusing, like the start of a film, or a cryptic clue in a spy drama.

I'm intrigued by the thought that, in his search for photographs of these particular cloud formations, V.H. Hurst went to the trouble of placing a small ad in the hope that someone might read it and miraculously have photographs of clouds from 23 June. He was then expecting to be sent photographic prints as a matter of course, no questions asked.

Why did he want the cloud photographs so desperately? Was it purely for his own research, or was he gathering information for something altogether more clandestine? These questions have bothered me ever since I came across this mysterious clipping. I'll probably never find out, but if you are reading this, Mr Hurst, please could you help me solve the mystery?

ANTHONY BURRILL

IF ANYONE photographed THE CUMULUS CLOUDS on June 23rd, please contact or send prints to V.H. Hurst, 26 Cliveden Road, SW19.

優質指示牌　　　永不褪色

電力危險

A generic warning sign is made much more interesting with the addition of Chinese characters. I'd hazard a guess that the characters spell out 'Danger!' or something similar. That's the beauty of non-verbal visual communication. The visual lightning-strike graphic warns everybody, even non-Chinese readers, that there is imminent danger.

The lightning-arrow graphic has its roots in an internationally recognized safety sign register. This ubiquitous graphic symbol is known and understood everywhere. Its jagged form and sharp pointed arrow visually represent the physical pain of receiving an electric shock.

Aside from its intended use as a warning sign, this graphic and ones similar to it have been co-opted by the wider graphic community to convey something potentially shocking and explosive. From rock music to a computer virus, this warning sign is synonymous with apparent danger.

It's fascinating how an arrangement of geometric forms can come to represent hazard through graphic means. Visual storytelling in its simplest form. Watch out, don't touch, danger is all around.

The umbrella as a visual metaphor is hard to avoid. How did this happen? It must have been after the umbrella had become widely adopted as a means of shelter from rain.

I find umbrellas compelling accessories: they provide protection from the elements, but also create an opportunity for human interaction. Sharing one with somebody you don't know is an intimate experience. You acknowledge your need to keep dry and are happy to invade each other's personal space for a few moments. The normal rules of society are temporarily put on hold.

I like the unintended surrealism of the oversized umbrella shown here. Umbrellas are inherently surreal objects that often appear in paintings by Belgian master Magritte. They conjure ideas of everyday objects taking on new life in a strange, imagined reality. Maybe it's to do with their dramatic transformation of form, or the way they blow inside out at just the wrong moment.

Drops of rain fall from the sky, and the precious cargo must be protected from the damaging elements. But what could be hidden inside to justify this special treatment?

ANTHONY BURRILL

By air mail
Par avion

PLACE
POSTAGE
STAMP
HERE

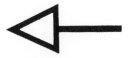

Place your postage stamp here; not over there, but right here. If the stamp is not placed in the correct position your postcard home will not be delivered. Your family will never hear of the beautiful things you have seen or the wonderful people you have met. Whole chapters of your life will be forgotten if you place the stamp in the wrong place. Obey the instructions; they are there for your own good.

How much longer will we use postage stamps? It seems like their time is almost up. Surely there are much simpler ways of sending short messages than posting letters and cards to each other? But still they are used and are incredibly romantic. They speak of a different time, when postal stamps represented the cutting edge of technology – as novel as an email or an emoji-encrusted text message is today.

But you can't keep a text message in a shoe box under your bed as a reminder of a love affair that ended too soon. Well, maybe you could print out the message on an A4 piece of office paper. Not quite as charming, is it?

I picked up this announcement from the pavement of Shaftesbury Avenue in the heart of London's theatre district, sometime in the early 1990s. It must have been discarded by a theatre-goer after a performance. I was drawn to the simple approach to design and layout. A typewriter has been used to type out the information in a no-nonsense manner.

There is an honest beauty about the small scrap of paper; the information is communicated with the minimum of fuss. But like so many things, what is actually said isn't in the words that are written but in what is left out. We can read between the lines that this was a last-minute change to the cast of the play. 'Indisposed' is a vague term that can suggest many things. Was Miss Baker genuinely ill, or had she had second thoughts about her performance that evening?

I've tried to research the people mentioned in this announcement, but I can't identify the play or when it was performed. Maybe this scrap had been lodged out of sight for years and only recently uncovered, finally revealing its message to the world.

ANTHONY BURRILL

We regret to announce
that Miss Hylda Baker
is indisposed

The part of Mrs Piper
will be played by
Miss Justine Elliott
at this performance
and the part of Marian
Selby by Miss Jacqueline
Grieve

NOW

REDUCED

NOW

REDUCED

NOW

REDUCED

NOW

REDUCED

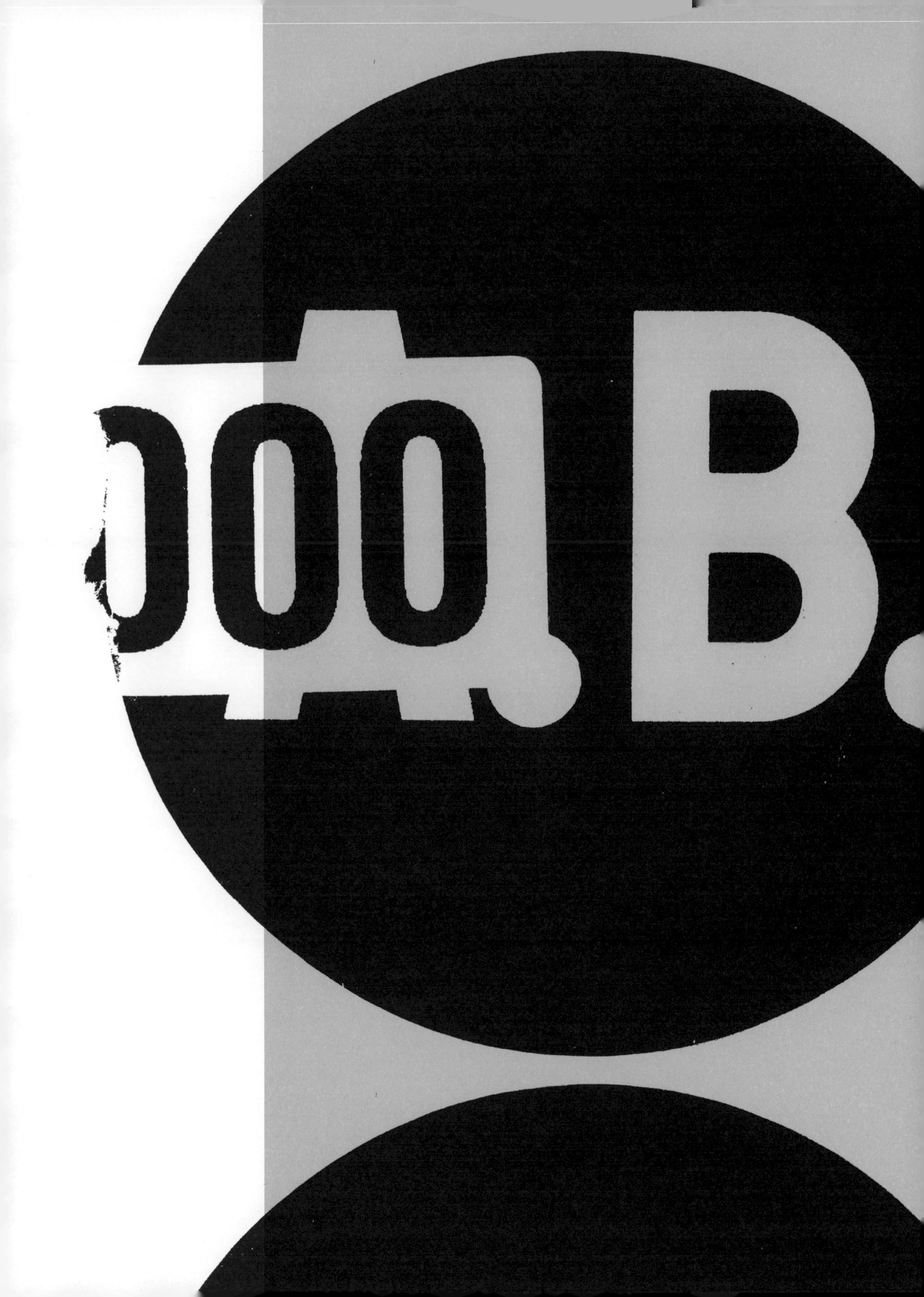

I've broken my own rules, but rules are meant to be broken.

This isn't a piece of found ephemera, it's some of my own work. I say my own work, but most of the design existed already. The original line of text read 'Watch out! There's a thief about.' The sticker was part of a crime prevention campaign, and was used widely in print and TV advertising when I was growing up. I was always slightly disturbed by the drawing of the escaping criminal. His jacket flapping in the wind and his heeled boots made him look more like a pop star than a desperate law breaker fleeing from the scene of the crime.

So I took the original design and – I thought – somewhat cleverly switched things around so it read 'Watch out! There's an artist about.' I know, it sounds slightly corny, doesn't it? The idea of an artist as someone who is above the law, an exciting figure something like a cross between a highwayman and a superhero. Of course it was meant as a visual joke; I knew that artists weren't really the mysterious figures of the popular imagination. They were people like me. People who observe reality through the lens of creative thinking and re-present it transformed. Showing how things really are, rather than how they appear.

Or maybe it was just lucky that I had the right letters to spell out 'artist'.

ANTHONY BURRILL

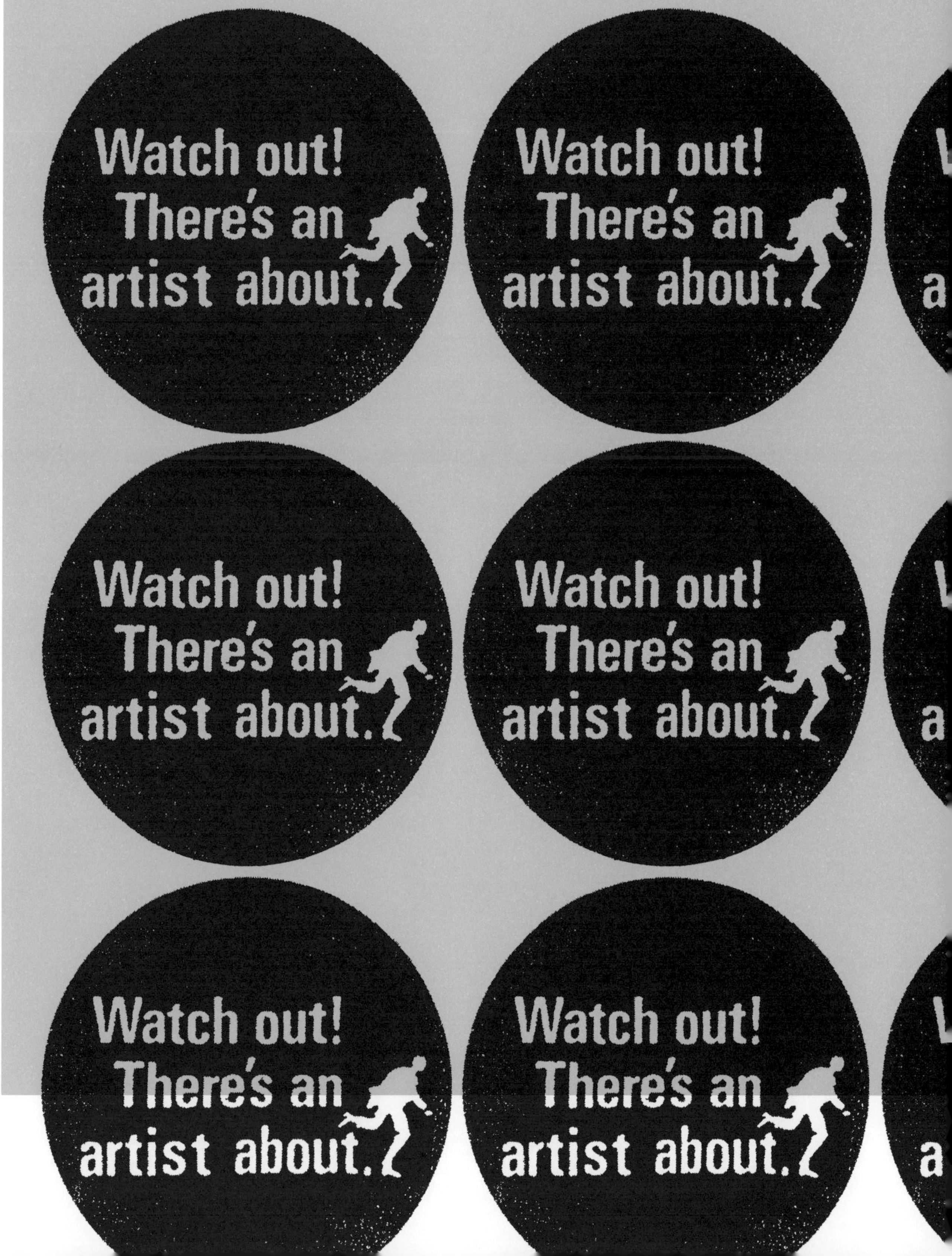

THE GUARDIAN
Friday January 20 1989

Gurus in Vermont

One of the most interesting differences is that Menshikov sees the welfare state as a sort of socialist Trojan horse in the

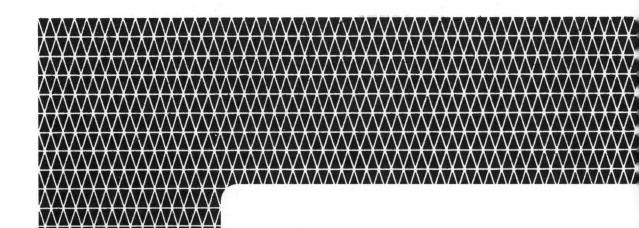

Where were you on 20 January 1989?

I know where I was.

I was at home reading a fascinating article in the Guardian newspaper about 'Gurus in Vermont'. I know this because I must have been so interested in the article that I cut the headline out of the newspaper and kept it in my sketchbook. It was just the headline I was interested in, because I didn't keep the rest of the article.

The unexpected nature of the headline grabbed my attention. Who were the Gurus, and what were they doing in Vermont? I still like the ambiguity of the headline; it's tempting us with its mysterious visual allusion. The collision of two worlds neatly summed up in a short phrase. It could be the title of a book or film; a tale of the cosmic meeting with the everyday.

This price ticket tells a short story all of its own.

A metaphorical final act where the discount is the only winner.

What was 81p is now 75p.

A saving of six pence (if my maths is correct).

It's the end of the range, there will be no more after this final reduction.

It's all over.

You can buy it now for 75p, but even that won't last for long.

You haven't got much time left.

Buy it now.

Grab it while you can.

It's a bargain.

Think of the saving.

But don't think too long, because it's almost over.

Too late.

You waited too long.

It's gone now.

That was the end of the range.

ANTHONY BURRILL

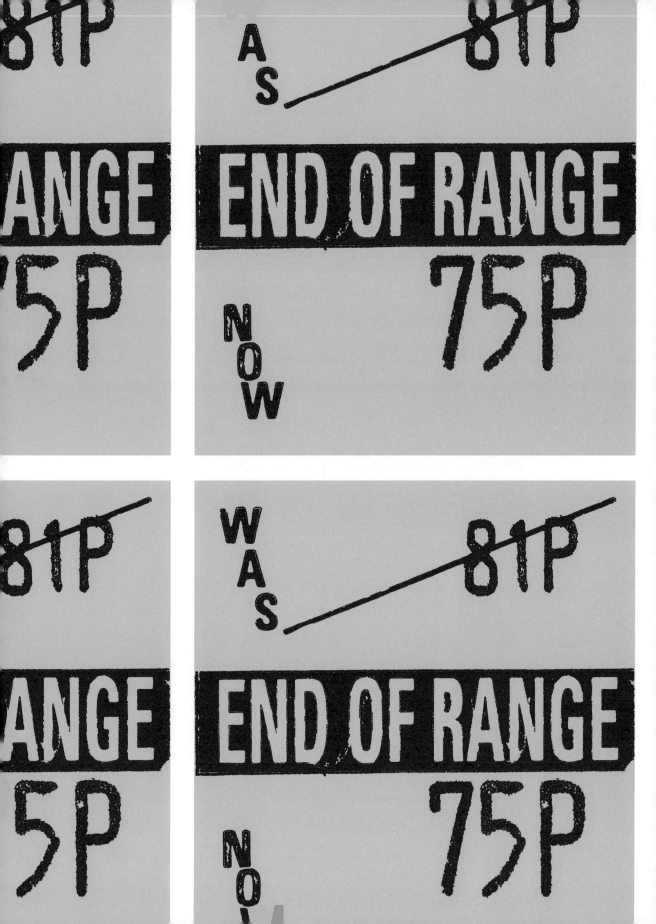

NEW
COMPUTERS

IN THE INTEREST OF PROVIDING A MODERN,
EFFICIENT SERVICE TO OUR CUSTOMERS WE ARE
INTRODUCING COMPUTERS INTO THIS OFFICE ON
23 JUNE.

They're here on 23 June, the new computers.

They're here to make all our lives simpler and more efficient.

They'll answer all our questions.

They'll solve all our problems.

On 24 June we'll witness a new and more modern world.

This office will run like clockwork; we will finally be freed from the mundane chores of life without computers.

They'll be here on the 23rd, there's nothing to be afraid of.

Evidence here of the dawn of the computer age; nothing would escape the information technology revolution. From here on in we would all play our part in the new age of technology. At least that was the idea. What actually happened was slightly less exciting. The queue at the Post Office has remained the same length.

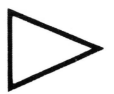

Do not bend it, fold it or force it through a narrow letterbox. The contents of this package are fragile and should be handled with care. Please, don't be tempted to crush the contents or mangle the delicate material contained within.

ANTHONY BURRILL

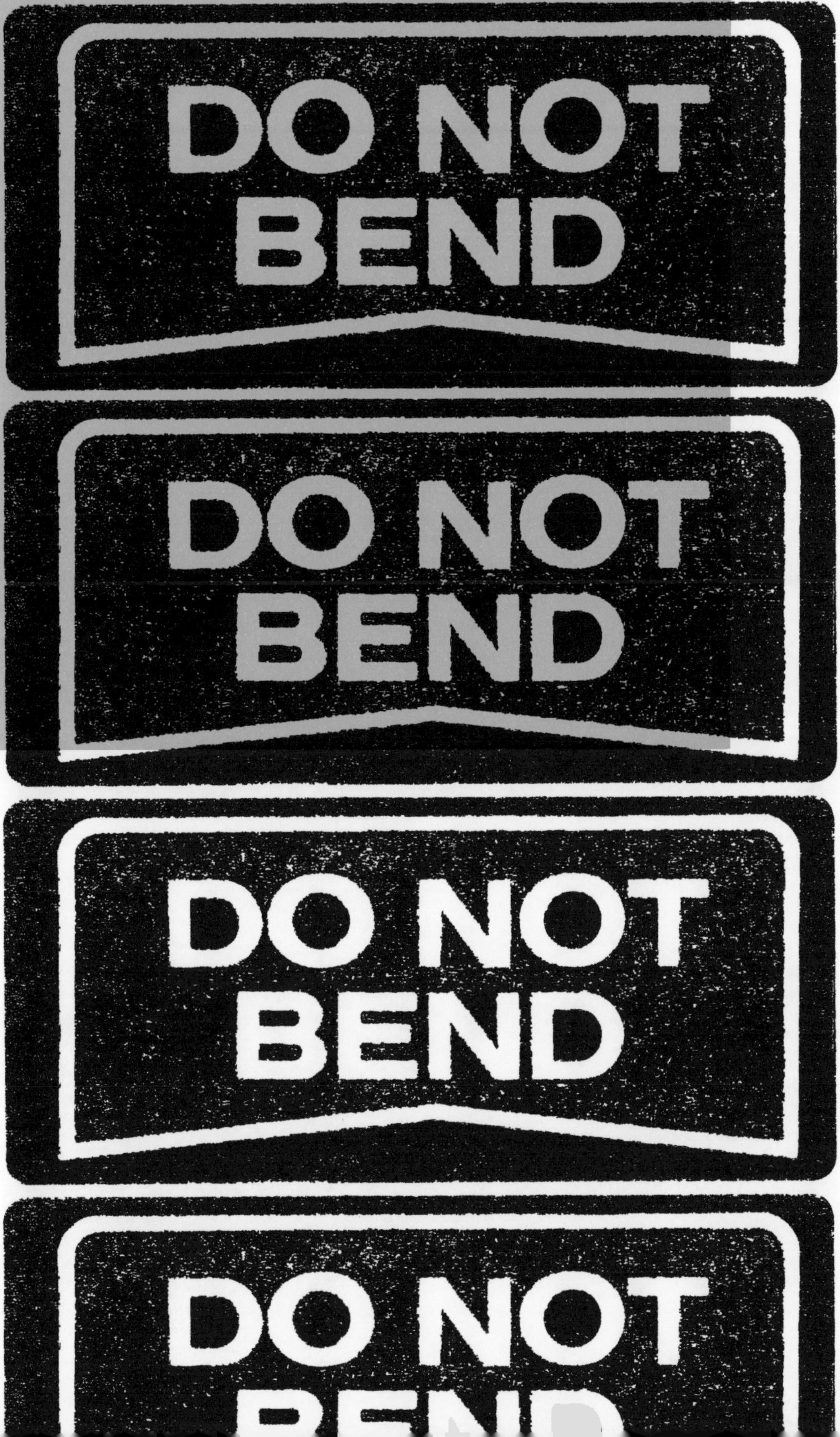
DO NOT BEND
DO NOT BEND
DO NOT BEND
DO NOT

COPY COPY

COPY COPY

COPY COPY

COPY COPY

COPY COPY

COPY COPY

ORIGINAL ORIGI

ORIGINAL ORIGI

ORIGINAL ORIGI

ORIGINAL ORIGI

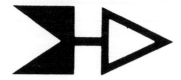

In this age of perfect smartphone photography, it's hard to imagine your snaps being anything less than perfect. But in the days of analogue cameras the thrill you felt when receiving prints back from the photo lab is hard to describe. How would the birthday party pictures turn out? Would everyone have red eye? Would we all be in focus? Developing your roll of film was an act of faith.

It was expensive, too, and time consuming. Most labs offered a basic seven-day service, or if you were in a hurry you could get the photos back overnight. But that was the expensive option, and nobody was really in such a hurry in those days. We all accepted that there would be a long gap between taking the photographs and seeing the results of our artistry.

When you finally got the prints back, how they turned out was a lottery. Some would be pin sharp and perfectly exposed, while others would be foggy and blurred. The helpful technicians in the lab would fix advice labels to shots that didn't measure up to their exacting standards. Helpful tips such as guidance on shutter release times would be stuck to the front of your disappointing images.

This felt quite intrusive, though they meant well. After all, they only wanted us to take better photographs.

ANTHONY BURRILL

QUALITY CONTROL
Prints too dark - underexposed
Where possible use slower shutter speed/flash/larger
lens aperture or faster film speed
Prints too light - overexposed
Where possible use faster shutter speed/smaller lens
aperture or slower film
In all cases refer to camera/film guide
ADVICE LABEL

LIFT & PEEL HERE

'Spot the ball' is a curious competition featured in tabloid newspapers. You play by marking an 'x' on a photograph of a football match where you think the ball is most likely to be. The ball in question has been airbrushed out, leaving only an empty patch of sky and a footballer at full stretch for reference. Accurately marking the position of the football wins you a cash prize.

How could the odds of spotting the ball be shortened in your favour? This is where a handy rubber stamp of repeated 'x' marks comes in. Simply stamp all over the photograph, and you are bound to win.

Well, that's the theory. I don't know if anybody was ever successful using this cunning method. I saw an advertisement for the rubber stamp and was intrigued by the idea. So I sent off a cheque and within a few days received the stamp.

Sadly I never used it to enter a spot the ball competition, and didn't win any star prizes. However I have used it in the name of art, decorating mail art envelopes and creating interesting overlapping patterns.

This kind of intricate diagram comes with any new electrical plug to give you important safety information for wiring the plug. Green and yellow to earth, blue or black to neutral, and brown or red to live. As you can see, there is no room for error; this is potentially a matter of life and death.

As well as its life-saving function, this small piece of printed card also works as a beautiful abstract design. The curved lines of the wires connecting to the terminals are extremely satisfying to look at. It resembles an aerial view of a futuristic town delineated in fine, precise lines.

ANTHONY BURRILL

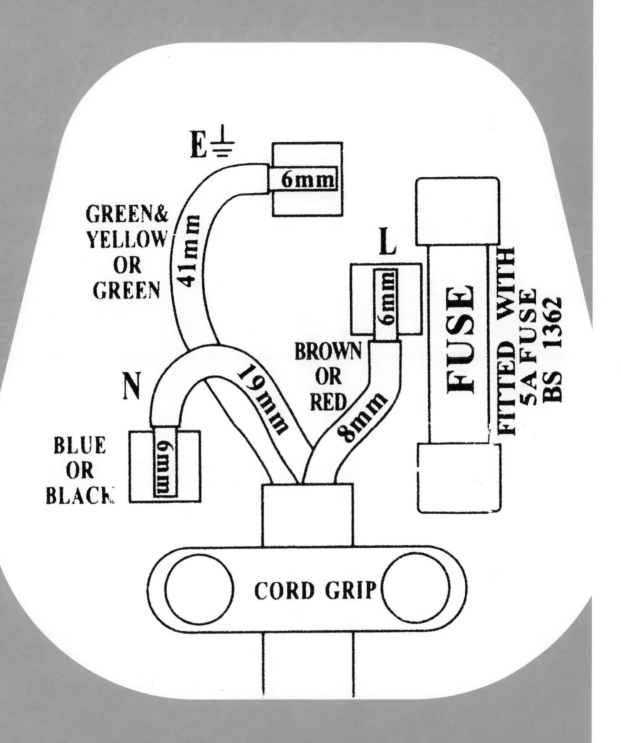

	7255	DATE	PERSONS	TABLE	WAITER

FANELLI'S
CAFE

94 PRINCE ST., N.Y., N.Y. 10012 (212) 226-9412

20

2213

5 74

3	1	9	1	9	6		5	7	4	c

This is another treasured find from my first trip to New York. I love everything about this till receipt. The classic typography was no doubt inspired by the Vignelli-designed subway map, with its austere use of the modernist grid and the beautiful left-ranged typography. Even in this humble scrap the quality of great design is evident. Attention to detail is key when working with such simplicity.

My parents placed this marriage announcement in the local newspaper of my home town, the Oldham Evening Chronicle. My wife and I married in Las Vegas, and this was my mother's way of telling the world. Emma and I are both graduates of the Royal College of Art; my mother was hugely proud of this, and quoted our qualifications at any opportunity.

This tiny announcement was the equivalent of posting on social media. The local newspaper was still widely read in my home town at the time, and was the primary source for finding out who had been born, who had got married and who had died.

As a side note, I'm drawn to the awkward typesetting and choice of typeface, reminiscent of letterpress.

ANTHONY BURRILL

Hope's Sportscards and Stationery

合 成 文 具

(415) 885-0955

1368 Pacific Avenue
San Francisco, CA 94109

MARRIAGES

BURRILL — PARKER — Announcing the marriage of Anthony Burrill M.A. R.C.A. and Emma Parker M.A. Dis. R.C.A. On March 9, 1996, at the Graceland Chapel, Las Vegas U.S.A.

LT928

Sometimes it's not possible to physically acquire great examples of street graphics, for example when they're carved out of stone and securely fixed to a wall. In these cases it's better to take photographs and remember them that way.

LOOK & SEE

It's difficult not to take photographs when you're at an airport. A huge temptation is to take a snap of a departure board or an aircraft and post it on social media. I try to avoid that as much as possible; however, I am always drawn to the amazing abstract designs you see on painted on the runways and taxiways.

ANTHONY BURRILL

The jagged lines, directional arrows and hard-to-decipher lettering are a real treat for the travelling designer. So I find myself capturing interesting abstract details, mainly for my own satisfaction, though the odd picture does appear on social media – and for that I apologize.

LOOK & SEE

Whenever I visit a friend's studio or have a meeting in an interesting building I'm drawn to the physical fabric of the place: its textures, patterns and wayfinding markings.

ANTHONY BURRILL

Sometime I arrive late for meetings, distracted, because I've spotted an interesting letterform or nice tile pattern.

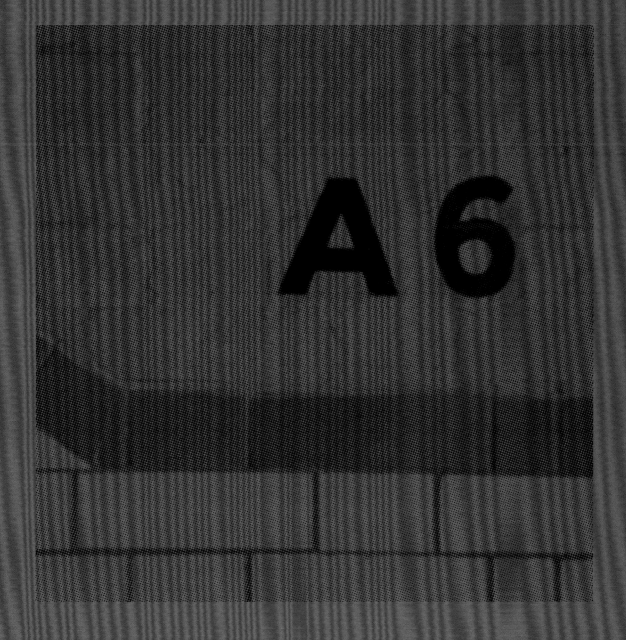

Even the most mundane things can look exotic when they are unfamiliar. Especially when I'm travelling I look out for generic signage and graphics that may be familiar to the people living locally, but to me they present a whole new visual language to explore.

ANTHONY BURRILL

With the added bonus of being written in a foreign language, words and letters acquire even more mystery and allure.

Multi-storey car parks are a source of endless fascination to me. I find their language of space and function interesting. Their crude edges impart a brutal quality. Concrete is rough hewn; stairwells are echoey and brightly lit.

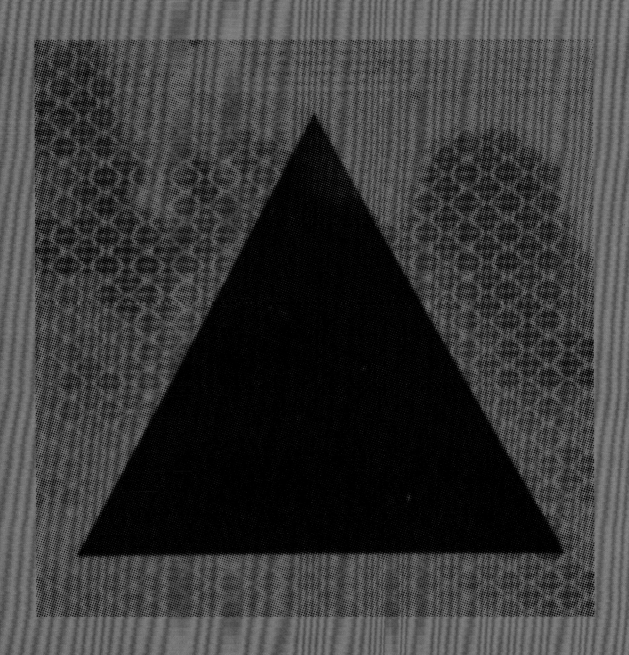

ANTHONY BURRILL

The wayfinding graphics are an extension of street graphics but spelt out in starker terms. The signs are larger, the arrows more acute. There is the sense of a heightened graphic landscape that I find thrilling.

Industrial estates on the margins of cities are unloved, liminal spaces. Designed purely for function and attacked daily by hostile conditions, there are rich pickings to be had there for the brave graphic explorer.

ANTHONY BURRILL

CCTV and security guards patrol these spaces. I've been asked numerous times for the reason I'm taking pictures of rusting signs and hand-painted notices. I explain what I'm interested in, and why I find it fascinating. This is met with a mixture of disbelief and puzzlement, and I'm usually left alone after that.

LOOK & SEE

I seek out overlooked survivals of former signage and traces of evidence left by people. Ancient graffiti in historic buildings is fascinating. I get a strange feeling when I see someone's carved initials dated hundreds of years in the past.

ANTHONY BURRILL

Spotted in a doorway, this mosaic letter A is part of a long closed-down shop, its once-grand entranceway now shabby and fragmented. The letterform is beautiful; the sharp angles of the incised tiles make it both bold and delicate. A bitmapped typeface created a hundred years ago.

LOOK & SEE

Faded hand-painted signage is hugely fascinating, and has become quite well documented. There are always interesting remnants of forgotten lettering on old shop fronts.

ANTHONY BURRILL

The skill employed in this kind of lettering is incredible, with each sign painter developing a unique approach to the craft.

Sun-baked tarmac enhances the splendid deterioration of painted letterforms, battered by vehicle tyres and scrubbed by the elements. They take on a painterly look and feel when observed in close-up.

ANTHONY BURRILL

Opening up an old sketchbook is fascinating; it contains material from long-forgotten trips and projects. It's the stuff that isn't important enough to be featured anywhere else, but tells an alternative story.

Reminders of places you've been to and things you've seen, these physical artefacts connect you directly to a time and place that photographs can't.

This kind of material is easy to collect; it's cheap, sometimes free and always easily available. It's lightweight and portable, lives happily inside a sketchbook and provides enduring inspiration.

The weather is changeable, closing in.
Will the sun shine or will the wind blow?
Our little home braves the elements,
standing firm against the weather, fair
or foul.

ANTHONY BURRILL

NO. 24 **Roman** 1 inch (APPROX. 25 mm) CAPS AND NUMBERS

ABCDEF
GHIJKL
MNOPQS
RSTUV★
WXYZ?-
123456
789;!&¢

Com Inc.
1207 Bernard Drive Baltimore, Md 21223   Made in U.S.A   well spaced professional lettering

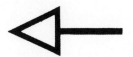

There are numerous variations on the design of stencil typefaces, and I'm always on the lookout for new additions to my collection. When travelling for work or on holiday I seek out hardware stores to find interesting examples of signage and typography. I like to collect physical examples of type that has an unusual quality or shows signs of its manufacturing process.

This example was found in a hardware store in Los Angeles. The way in which the card has been die-stamped to produce the letterforms is quite crude, and some of the edges of the material have been torn. This gives the resulting typeface a rough-hewn quality that I like. It isn't perfect, and this is the very quality that I look for.

The stencil sheet also boasts a handy measuring guide in both metric and imperial units.

I find type examples in the most unusual places. My car had been serviced at the local garage, and the mechanic had left a piece of paper in the footwell to protect the car against dirt and oil. Most people would screw this up and throw it away, but I carefully folded it up and took it home.

The reason for my care and attention was the unusual typeface that had been used as part of the design. The letterforms come from a simple blocky design based on tall rectangles. The corners of the letters have been slightly rounded, but the rest of the detail is thrillingly sparse.

The coarse texture of low-quality printing combined with a rough choice of paper stock makes for a brutal lo-fi quality. Naturally I've thought about designing a complete typeface based on this template. It would be quite simple to develop a complete character set from this example. Another project to add to my 'to do' list.

ANTHONY BURRILL

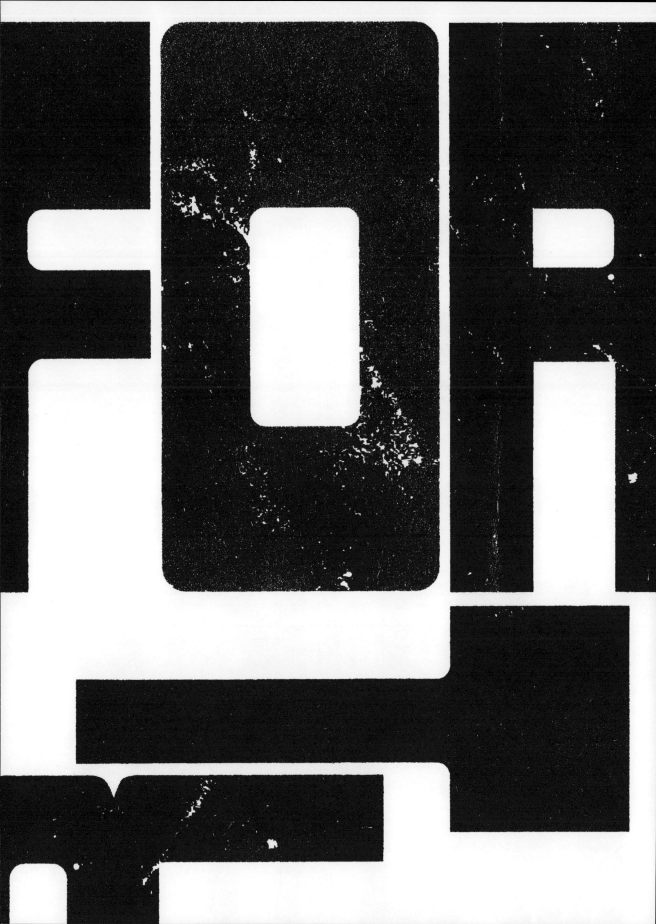

A B C D
E F G H
J K L
M N O P

These ubiquitous self-adhesive letters were found in my local DIY store. I bought the complete alphabet and numerals for a project I was working on. It was a poster for a music festival in the Netherlands, and this typeface was the perfect choice for the job. To make sure I had all the letters I needed I made a layout of the poster on the concrete floor of the store. It was a good way to design the layout. I tried combining a large size and small size together, and even tried some italic letters for variety.

The other shoppers in the store ignored my attempts to turn the signage aisle into a temporary design studio. Once I was satisfied with the layout and that I had enough letters I bought them and took them home. This was in pre-computer days, so I glued the letters to thick card to produce the final poster design. I then posted the completed typographic construction to Amsterdam, where the festival poster was printed.

LOOK & SEE

This peculiar series of illustrations
are a detail from a guide to exposures
found on the inside of a box of 35mm
photographic film. Each 'f-stop'
is illustrated in different lighting
conditions: full sun, semi-shade and
full shadow.

I am fascinated by these spooky
miniature scenes designed primarily
to aid successful photography,
but suggesting to me an unfolding
Hitchcockian psycho-drama. Who are
the people in the drawings, and why
is the man taking photographs of the
woman? The suggestion of landscape
feels almost surreal with its perfect
rolling hills and constant sunlight.
The stark geometry of the building
disrupts the rural idyll, maybe hinting
at the darker nature of this particular
photographic assignment.

ANTHONY BURRILL

frag

frag

frag

34567

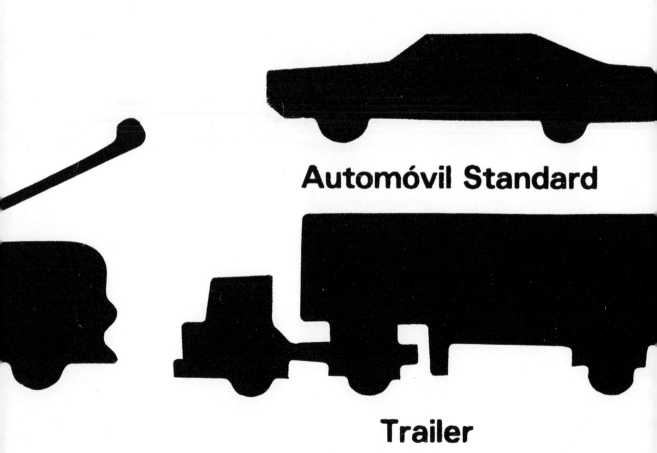

Automóvil Standard

Trailer

Autobús

Locomotora

M.I.R.   *HECHO EN MEXICO*

SPECIAL

OFFER

£1:99

SPECIAL

OFFER

£1:99

SPECIAL

OFFER

£1:99

I also collect print samples and layout guides. I savour these examples of design where options are limited. Choose your address label in a standardized five-line arrangement of either Helvetica or Helvetica Bold. It's a liberating feeling when all other design choices are off-limits. You can either choose bold or regular, that's it.

Limitations are good for the design process. When you have unlimited choice it's difficult to focus on one thing. By taking away all but the essential options you give yourself boundaries. When you have very little to work with you have to be ingenious and resourceful with your choices, which makes for much leaner and more interesting solutions.

ANTHONY BURRILL

NE

**STIK-ADDRESS
STANDARD FIVE LINE
GOLD LABEL IN
HELVETICA AND
HELVETICA BOLD**

NE

**STIK-ADDRESS
STANDARD FIVE LINE
GOLD LABEL IN
HELVETICA AND
HELVETICA BOLD**

NE

**STIK-ADDRESS
STANDARD FIVE LINE
GOLD LABEL IN
HELVETICA AND
HELVETICA BOLD**

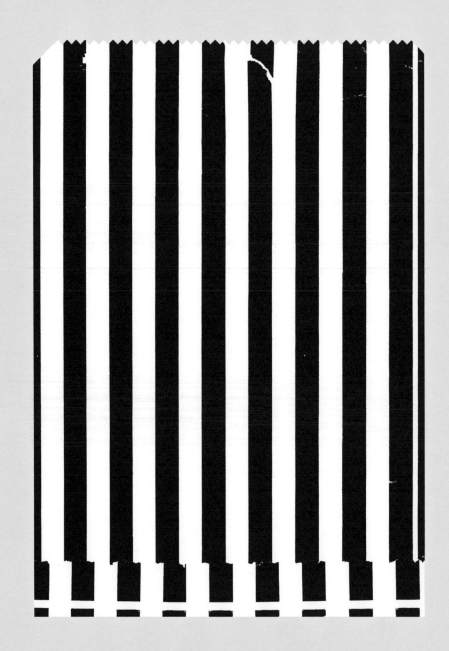

This is a particularly beautiful example of a generic paper bag; I think this one is from a local sweet shop. The candy stripes and lightweight paper stock make it ideal for small stationery items or a handful of pear drops. The ephemeral nature of the bag makes it even sweeter; its sole purpose to provide temporary packaging, its life span only expected to last a few minutes.

By studying the construction of the bag we can detect the signs of the manufacturing process. The way the serrated edge is crudely torn and the folds along the bottom give the bag a rough, handmade feel.

The distinctive stripes resemble tiny minimalist artworks; the dazzle pattern created by the folds of the bag disrupts the simplicity, creating movement and interest. It reminds us of deckchair patterns, seaside, sunshine and pleasure.

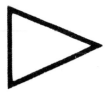

I got up early on 17 April 1989 to catch a train from Leeds to London. This was the day I had my interview at the Royal College of Art for a place on the MA graphic design course. I didn't know it at the time, but this journey was the beginning of my life in London and the start of my career in design.

At the time I must have realized it was a significant moment because I kept the ticket in my sketchbook. (The truth is I kept everything I picked up.) I was on the lookout for anything to stick in my sketchbook to help complete my visual diary. The notebooks I kept were my main focus at the time, and I became an expert in page layouts and double-page spreads.

Looking back, I think this is where I learnt most about handling type and images. Collage has always been central to my working practice, and this is where first I began to understand the skill of combining words and type.

BR 3502/

Reserved

Class	Coach	Seat
	D	56
BACK	to direction of travel	

Between

LEEDS ...
KINGS CROSS

0823 HGT-KGX
17 APR 89

R 188826

ONE HALF TO BE RETAINED

1

ADM

or

ALMEX CONTRO

I love the experience of going to the cinema to watch a film. The ritual of buying a ticket and finding your seat are all part of the build-up to the main event. I don't mind what I see, from art house to blockbuster; I savour that time away from the real world, transported to a different reality.

This simple paper ticket is from a small independent cinema in Leeds, close to the student house I shared with five friends. I would go and see everything that came out, good and bad. I can't remember which film this ticket was for, but I do remember the old-fashioned ticket machine. Once you had paid, your ticket would spool out of the machine with a clank.

You would take your ticket and hand it over to the manager on the door of the auditorium, who would then tear it in half and give you a crumpled fragment back in return. The fuzzy print on the ticket was barely legible, but that wasn't a problem. It was an archaic system even then.

It's intriguing to see a listing for a hypnotist alongside small ads for hairdressers and caravans for sale. These listings were found in the back pages of the local newspaper when I was a student in Leeds. It struck me as odd that such esoteric activities were advertised among other more mundane things.

To scan the column of text and come across an ad for a clairvoyant was also a surprise. Almost like entering a parallel universe where magical practices were an everyday occasion, just like selling your car or having your nails done.

I love the graphic feel of these ads; the way the text is compressed into a small space, the arrangement of upper-case bold and short lines of text. The inconsistency in the typesetting makes it a beautiful thing, with a texture that is highly appealing.

The graphic style of the ads feels like a camouflage to conceal the strangeness that's hidden within. An invisibility cloak that blurs the boundary between reality and imagination.

ANTHONY BURRILL

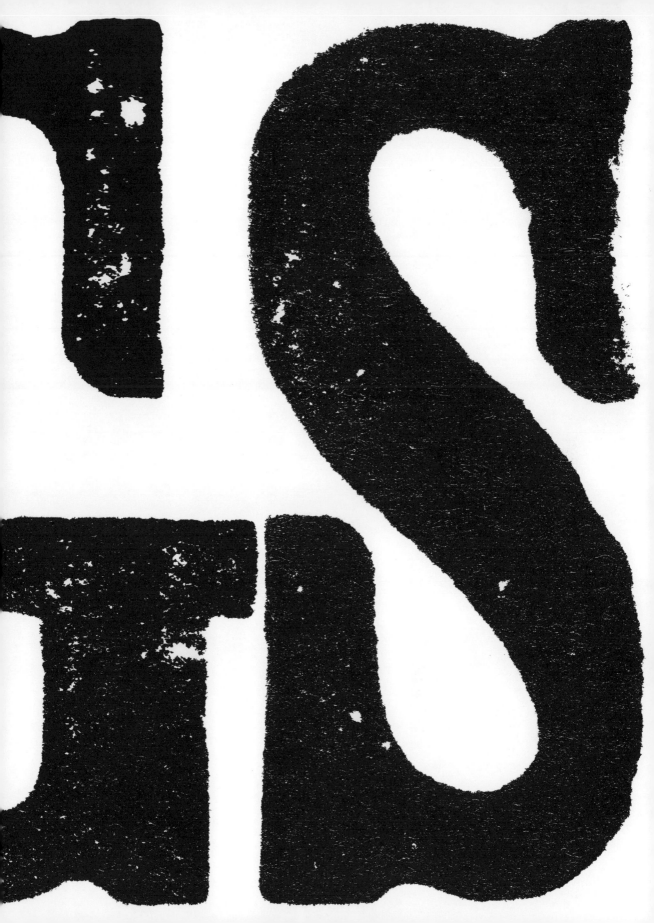

SCINTILLAS BOO

TASK MASTER

PORTLAND CAT

ANOTHER PINT

OLE MIO

ARINA

BACON

MULALADE

MONROE BAY

MBLE LASS

It's always a thrill to receive the 'Warning Paper Low' section of a till receipt. It feels as if your perfectly timed transaction has crept in just at the right moment, before the final whistle. You feel a moment of pity for the next person, and a little guilty. They will have to wait until the till roll has been replaced; a costly delay adding to the time already spent behind you in the queue.

But these feelings soon fade when you realize you have the prized possession, the final few centimetres of till roll, the special section clearly marked. The last rays of the sun as it dips behind the sea, darkness slowly gathering.

Tomorrow there will be a fresh new till roll, ready to spool out its never-ending stream of dot-matrix printed receipts. Little souvenirs of pocket money transactions.

ANTHONY BURRILL

PAPER LOW

WARNING:-
PAPER LOW

WARNING:-
PAPER LOW

WARNING:-
PAPER LOW

RN IS

3

YOUR TURN IS

C 7 6

YOUR

C

I picked this up while queuing. I can't remember where or when, but I do remember waiting a long time for my number to flash up on the LED display screen. The form and function of this piece of ephemera are firmly linked; when you tug on the ticket it tears away from the next ticket in turn. It's a satisfying feeling, so satisfying that I decided to grab a few extra tickets and stick them into my sketchbook.

The design of this ticket has become iconic. It's instantly recognizable to anyone who has ever had to wait in line for something. It might be in a supermarket, a doctor's surgery or anywhere that still operates this archaic system.

The arrangement of the typographic details is beautiful; the imperfection of the number stamp gives the ticket its unique look and feel. It is simultaneously mass produced and individually crafted – quite a feat for a humble piece of paper.

These shop door signs have been around for as long as I can remember; our constant companion along the high street. Nobody knows when, where or by whom they were designed.

I picked up my treasured copies of these shiny plastic signs in a corner shop in South London. All the old favourites were there on a rotating rack: Beware of the Dog, Keep Out, Exit, Private Property. The print had faded slightly and the plastic was yellowed with age.

The beautiful contrast between the script lettering and the more conventional condensed type is wonderfully satisfying. You feel that the signs really mean sorry or want you to come in; there is a humanity in the casual, friendly style of the lettering.

I took them home and they were proudly displayed in my makeshift studio. It was only when I later photocopied and deconstructed the signs that their true surrealist beauty became clear. I swapped the two top lines around so that the signs no longer made sense. 'Come in We're CLOSED', and the even more confusing 'Sorry We're OPEN' were suddenly revealed. I later made a screen print of this found artwork, which began to be used in various galleries and shops, confusing shoppers and delighting passersby in turn.

By taking the everyday and literally cutting and reassembling it, something new and interesting can be made.

ANTHONY BURRILL

SOUTHPORT ROCK

Ingredients: Sugar, glucose syrup, flavouring, colours
E122 E127 E142 E102 E132 & Brilliant Blue
SOUTHPORT ROCK CO. LTD., SOUTHPORT

Southport Rock isn't a music festival, it's a stick of super-sweet brightly coloured hard candy that's part of a day trip to the English seaside town. All British seaside towns have their own branded confectionery, with the town's name ingeniously running through the core of the extruded stick. Slipped in between the cellophane wrapping and the rod of pink sugar is a paper label.

This example comes from Southport in the northwest of England, not too far from where I grew up, and was collected on a drizzly midsummer day. The label's design is no-nonsense to say the least. A coarse halftone image of the promenade is featured alongside a list of delicious-sounding chemical ingredients. I'm drawn to the mysterious 'Brilliant Blue'; it isn't given an E number, just a name that sounds more like a gloss paint colour.

I love the stark functionality of this label; there's no branding, just pure information. I hope you had a happy day beside the seaside.

This is the way out, not the way in.

It's the EXIT.

The opposite of the entrance.

Don't try to come in this way.

It's the way out.

Do you want to come in?

Don't use this door.

This door leads to the outside, not
the inside.

If it's the inside you want, then you are
in the wrong place.

This is for the outside.

Not the inside.

This is not the way in, it's the way out.

ANTHONY BURRILL

EXIT

EXIT

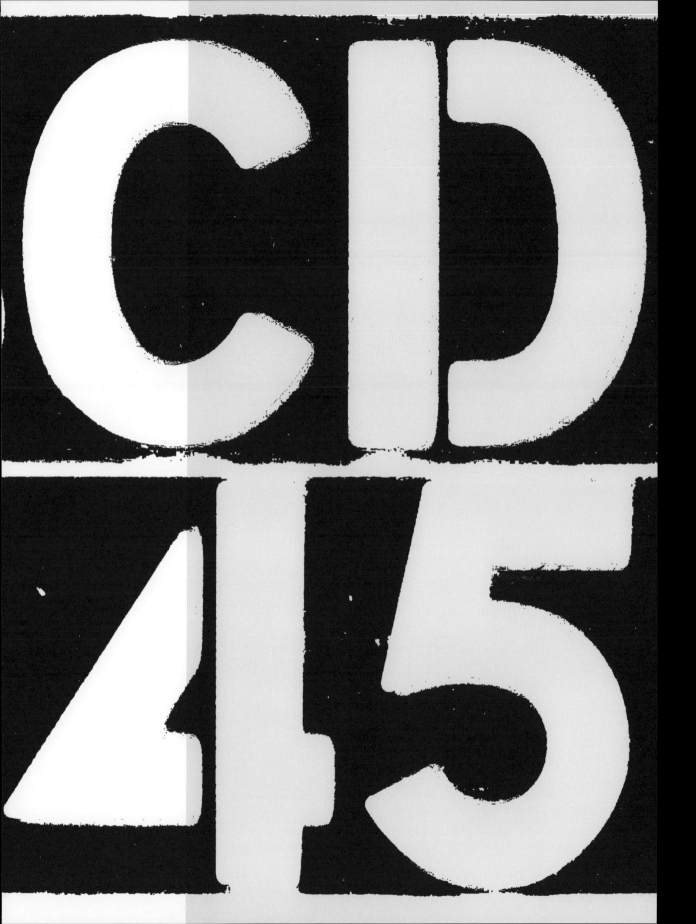

WEIGHT

5 Kg

WEIGHT

5 Kg

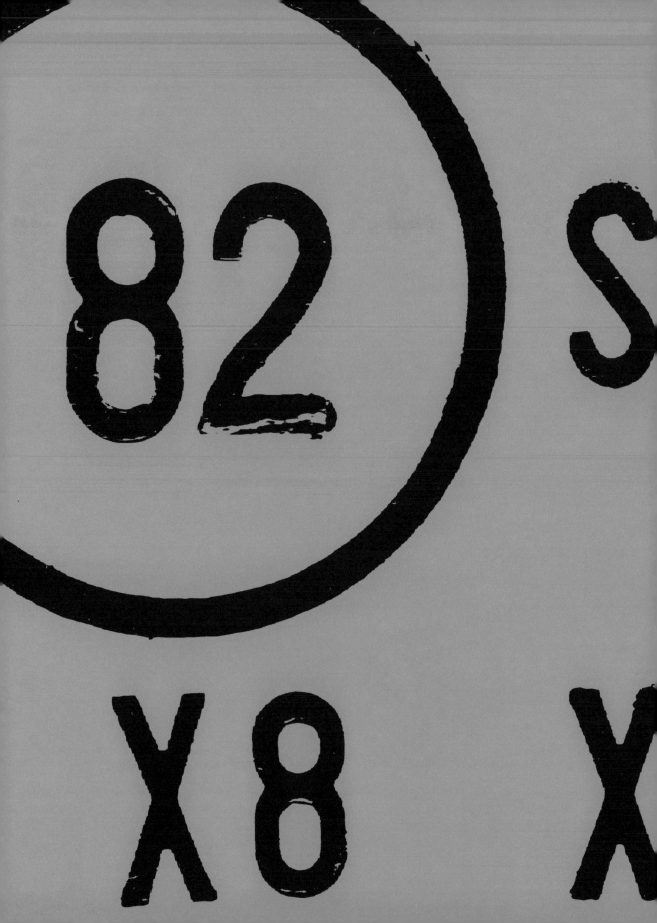

The graphic language of signs, stickers and tickets is fascinating and eclectic. It draws on the vast history of visual communication and then happily goes on to ignore it. It's a branch of design that seems to exist outside of taste and fashion.

This vernacular language has its own charm that ignores trends, and that's what makes it so interesting. It isn't concerned with being valued or admired, it's just doing a job.

Design like this, by non-designers, has always been of great interest to me. I love seeing evidence of how design rules are so easily broken or completely ignored.

Where to start? So many things going on in one place. Blackletter script combined with a digital-inspired typeface. This unconventional combination of type styles acts as a history lesson in type design. The medieval Gothic contrasts with the modern **LED** lettering in a jarring collage of joyous dissonance. These two type styles would not conventionally be seen together, but in the hands of the anonymous designer who conjured up this graphic magic they almost begin to work.

I cannot imagine the decisions that were made during the design process. Perhaps the client's brief asked for something timeless yet contemporary? This request was taken literally. Ancient and modern collide with thrilling results in this display of genre-defying visual communication.

Displayed with this prime example is a card with a more regular approach to the brief.

ANTHONY BURRILL

Albion Minicab Service

DRIVER(S) «» FULLY «» INSURED

CALL FREE **0800~163~174**

PARCEL SERVICE – REMOVALS
WEDDING CARS AVAILABLE
24 HOUR CAB SERVICE

0181-67 6639
0181-67 6630

NEW CAVEN JISH CARS

THE
RIGHT
KIND
OF
WRONG

Art and Construction by

ANTHONY BURRILL & MICHAEL MARRIOTT

MOTHER
The Biscuit Building
10 REDCHURCH STREET
LONDON E2 7DD

Thursday 15th January 2009
6.30 - 9.30 pm

PRINTED BY ADAMS OF RYE

This is the letterpress-printed invitation
to an exhibition I held in collaboration
with Michael Marriott in 2009. The
exhibition featured a large constructed
tower on wheels and wooden wall pieces
that married my typographic work with
Marriott's sculptural constructions.

The invitation's design reflected this
eclectic approach using a mixture
of type styles and sizes. I enjoyed the
process of producing this piece of work.
I had a rough idea of what I wanted
and spent the day searching through
drawers of wood and metal type at
Adams of Rye. Each line of text was
hand set in a different typeface, with
the final composition possessing a
collaged look and feel.

The resulting piece of print reflected
the visual look of the exhibition, but
also its underlying message about the
importance of truth and honesty, not
only in the choice of materials but
the way in which they are used and
the message they communicate. The
exhibition marked a significant turning
point in my career, when I chose to
focus more on my own projects rather
than working solely on commissions.

This repeat pattern of circles is made by a sheet of red dot stickers. In art exhibitions they are used to mark a piece of work that has been sold, by being stuck to the gallery wall next to the work that has been purchased. They are the markers of a successful artist; the more red dots you have next to your work, the more popular you are.

In the past they acted in the same way that 'likes' now work on social media. Gallery visitors can gauge how well the exhibition has gone by the number of red dots. It has been known for some artists to mark work that hasn't been sold with a red dot, in the hope that this will encourage people to invest in other works. Of course, I have never been guilty of this.

After my first few exhibitions I was left with lots of redundant sheets of red stickers, sales having not been as healthy as I'd hoped. I began making art with the left-over stickers, filling my sketchbooks with abstract compositions. I bought other stickers, some squares and rectangles, in a variety of bright colours to extend my palette.

These explorations of colour and geometry helped me to learn about composition and colour combinations; ideas I was to develop in my work. It's good to use unconventional materials to make work, with each medium having its own restrictions and possibilities.

ANTHONY BURRILL

PRESENT   A NITE OF

Action
NOT A BAG A MOUTH
Part Two

At Egypt Lawn, Johnstown
on Sat April 10, 1993
FEATURING

MELLO
STAR

VS DOCTOR SUD

Adm $20

REFRESHMENTS ON SALE

Letterpress and wood type has a unique character. The relationship between the letterforms and type styles produces interesting results. The in-built awkwardness of the type means that it sits together in an unusual and lively way. When typeset like this it feels full of life, vibrant and anarchic. This method of mixing typefaces and sizes is the result of necessity, and not necessarily a design process. The relaxed approach to spacing and composition feels like a party; it's a combination of lots of different characters from different backgrounds coming together to produce something unique.

This amazing poster was collected by my friend Tim when he was living in Jamaica. Letterpress was still used as the main printing method at the time. Its resilience and flexibility lent a distinctive visual look and feel to the dancehall culture on the island.

Tim has an enviable collection of these posters and flyers, each one unique and beautiful. It's a treat to see and handle the physical objects; their raw print quality is evocative, a souvenir from a particular time and place.

This beautiful, curvaceous ampersand is from the wood type collection at Adams of Rye, the local printer where I print letterpress posters. The ampersand is a mysterious character; it hangs around with other letterforms but represents a word. There is something different about ampersands: they're where type designers go to have fun.

There are numerous variations on the basic design. The looping and twisting of the letterform can be either complicated or straightforward. I like this ampersand because it's chunky, simple and bold. There is an echo of calligraphy in the form; you could just about imagine drawing it by hand with a quill pen. It's a bit battered, too, giving it a rugged charm and lived-in feel.

This ampersand has been around for years, joining other letters and words in many combinations.

ANTHONY BURRILL

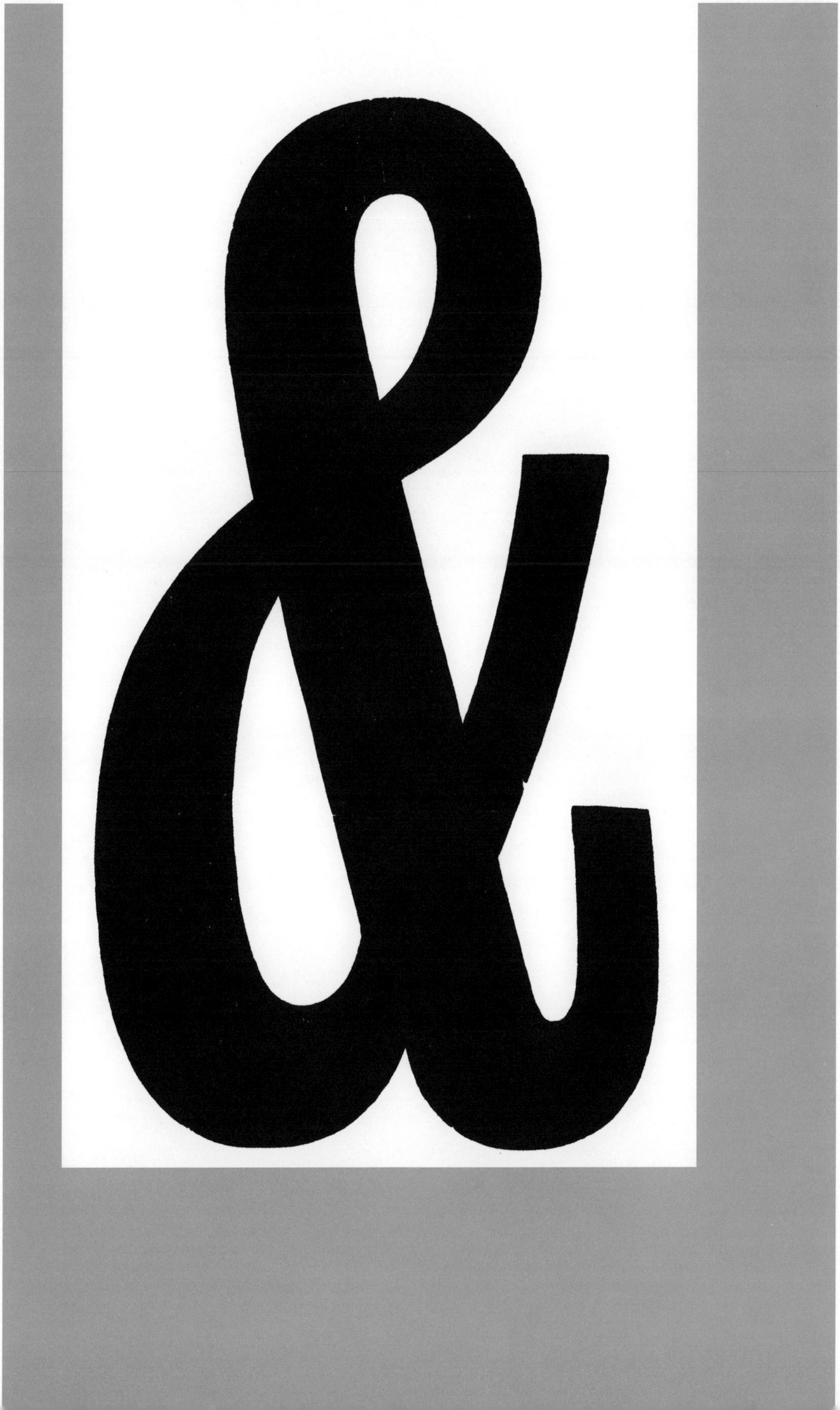

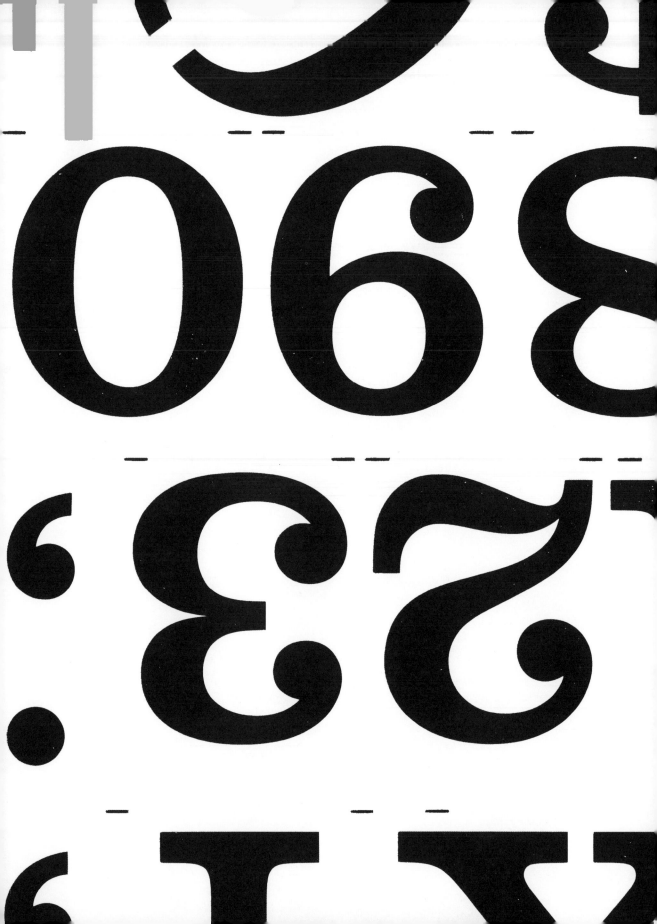

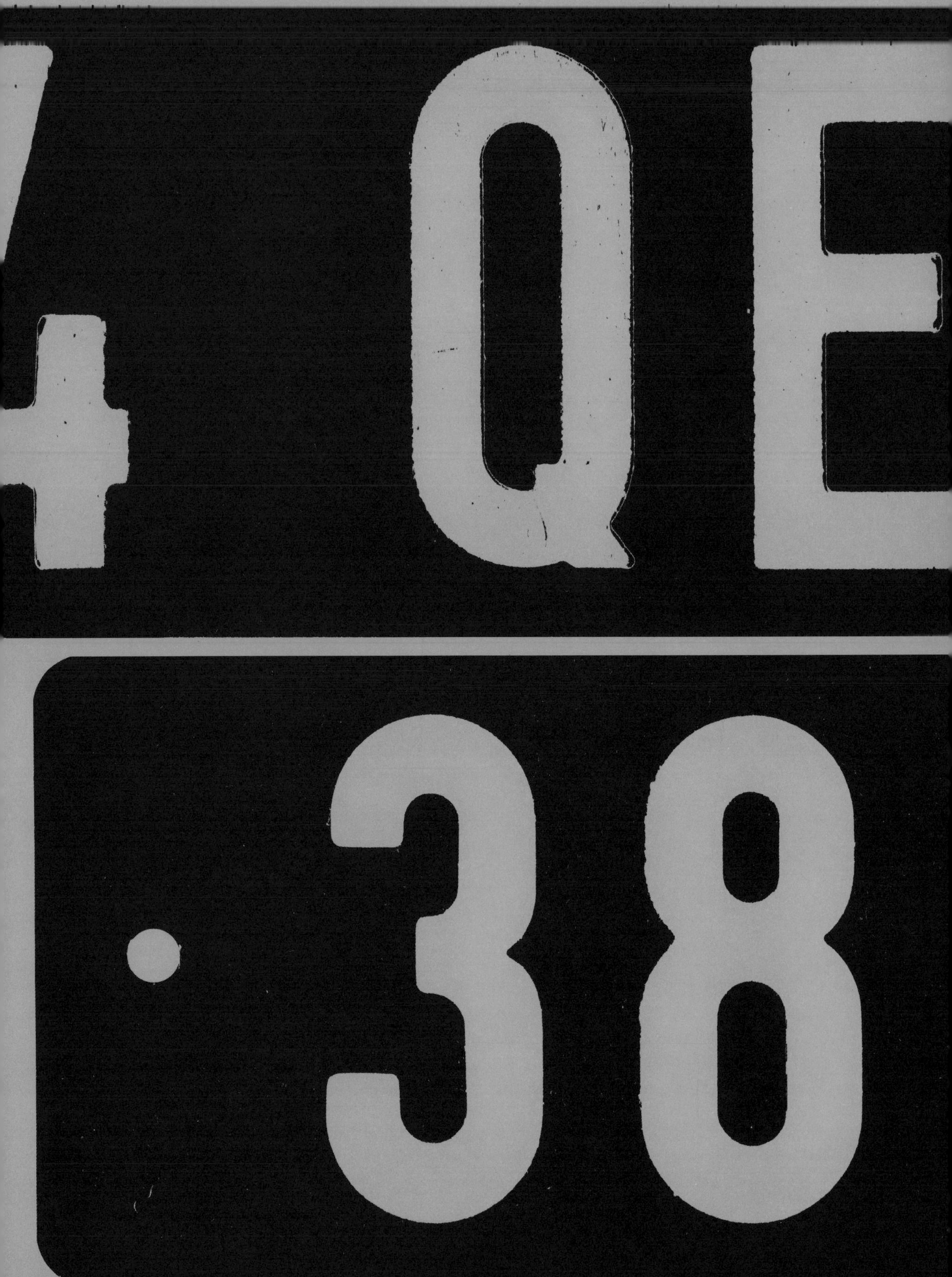
Q
38

72.

98.P

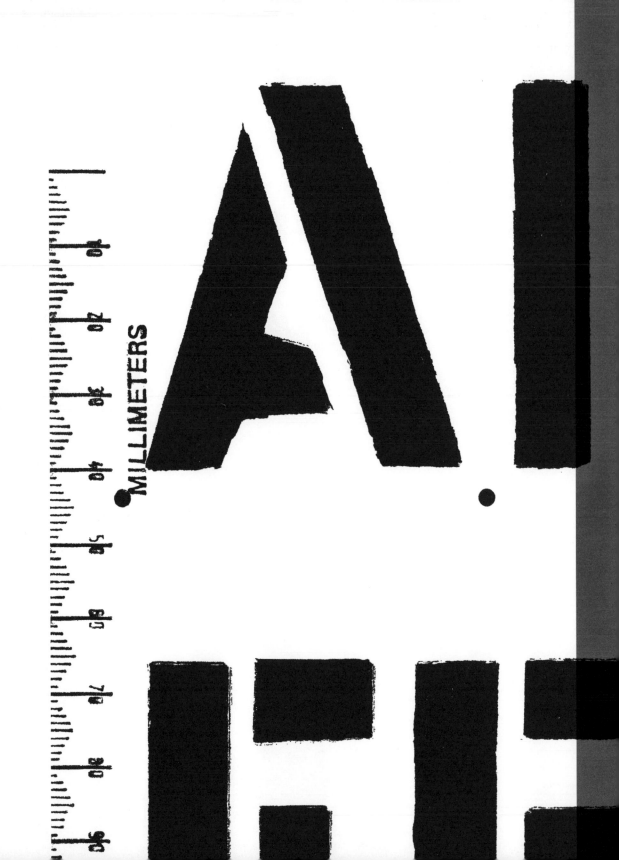

It might sound as if I travel just to find examples of interesting typography, unusual signs and interesting bus tickets. That's one of the reasons, but not the main one. I travel to see and experience new things, meet people and learn.

Recording these trips through photographs and collecting unconventional souvenirs is something I've always done naturally. It's part of my character to seek out this stuff and then feed it into my work as inspiration.

This beautiful poster was loosely attached to a wall in a side street in Barcelona when I noticed it. I simply had to brush past it, and the poster almost fell off the wall and into my hands by itself. It's as if it wanted to come home with me; I honestly had no choice in the matter.

ANTHONY BURRILL

A UN DÉCIMO
500 MILLONES
Décimos a
1000 Ptas.

中國民航

CAAC

登 机 牌
BOARDING PASS

经 济 舱
ECONOMY CLASS

航班 FLIGHT	日 期 DATE
目的地 DEST.	座 位 SEAT
	13c

684501

This boarding pass was for an internal flight in China that my grandfather and I took as part of our travels around the country. I went on many trips with him during my childhood, each time returning home with bags of postcards, museum guides, tickets and anything else I could collect. This is where my obsession with collecting began.

After every trip I would give an illustrated lecture about my travels to my friends at school. With each telling of my stories they would improve, becoming more interesting and exciting every time.

Learning these early lessons has formed me both as a person and a designer. My inquisitive nature was encouraged and cultivated by these trips.

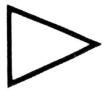

When viewed in isolation, a letterform resembles an abstract work of art. Divorced from its meaning, it can be enjoyed for its formal design and pleasing character. This letter E is a prime example. You can forget for a moment that it's the most hardworking letter of the alphabet, and admire the beauty of the design.

The condensed nature of the letterform adds to its statuesque proportions. The large slab serifs are countered by the more delicate design of the crossbar as it almost fills the internal space, creating interesting negative spaces.

This wood type example shows the wear of age, its corners softened and rounded. The wood has mellowed and scarred with use. The dents and cracks now give character to the printed word. A warmth and humanity comes through.

ANTHONY BURRILL

PITMANS GANG

O'MOLLY O

WHY DRY

SADUVA

POLLY'S CASE

ROWFOLD EARNEST

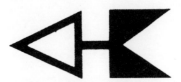

This letterpress printed sheet and two others like it were given to me by my friend Nigel. He found a stack of these poetic notices at Haringey Greyhound Stadium in the 1990s. Each race of the evening would have been billed in this way, displaying the names of the dogs racing. The list of names sounds like a poem; a haiku of unrelated abstract words, or a concrete poem of jumbled place names and images.

The roughness of the printing gives it the look and feel of an artwork, maybe a lost work by a Fluxus artist. It's a puzzling stream of consciousness; there's no beginning, middle or end, only a continuous, scrolling list of invented names. A real work of art.

This tiny label was attached to a replacement toner cartridge for the inkjet printer in my studio. Usually I rip off the labels and throw them away. This one is so small that the text is almost invisible to the naked eye. It was only when I looked closer that I saw the interesting collection of languages and type styles.

I'm drawn to these miniature pieces of design that exist on the margins. They are ignored most of the time, but quite beautiful when looked at again.

It's the vertical stack of type and the arrow that I like so much. Printed on a roll, it's a repeat. Communicating its message over and over again. I'm intrigued by repetition, and the way that something complicated can be made out of a small number of elements.

This little masterpiece of minimalism inspires me. Remove everything that isn't useful. Strip things down to the minimum, and true beauty will be revealed.

ANTHONY BURRILL

はか**す**
掲 **去**

REMOVE
RETIREZ
はが**す**
掲 **去**

REMOVE
RETIREZ

Special Delivery

Special Delivery

pecial Delivery

Special Delivery

pecial Delivery

Special Delivery

pecial Delivery

Special Delivery

pecial Delivery

Special Delivery

pecial Delivery

pecial Delivery

Special Delivery

pecial Delivery

Special Delivery

When the way up is the way down, where should we go? Signs and arrows are designed to be specific to their role. When that is subverted the sign becomes something else; it's useless for its primary function, but turns into something much more interesting.

By subverting signs and systems you can play with visual language. When does up mean down? When does down mean up?

I like to play with expectations and encourage people to question what they think through my work. We are told to follow instructions carefully, but when the sign points the wrong way, what are we meant to do? Follow it knowing that we are heading in the wrong direction, or go the way we know is wrong to find out something new?

ANTHONY BURRILL

WINDOW CLEA___
HAS CALLED
THANK YOU

The window cleaner has called; he has cleaned the windows. This card tells you that the windows have been cleaned, by the window cleaner.

Look through the window, the glass is clean. Much cleaner than before, when it was dirty and needed cleaning.

Roughly rubber stamped on a piece of card, this beautiful piece of visual communication tells you what you are reading before you have read it.

It is a pure visual idea; the dirty type has almost been cleaned away.

A prime example of function following form, or is it the other way around?

This sample of letterpress borders demonstrates the endless possibilities of geometric abstraction. Waves, zig-zags and smooth undulations create pleasing decorative elements to be used in graphic communication. One of the aims of my work is to reduce the amount of visual information to the minimum. To have just enough to say what I want to say. I concentrate on the message and try not to be seduced by unnecessary decoration.

When viewed in isolation like this, these graphic elements take on a significance they were never intended to have. They suggest endless variations, each one made by obeying the same laws but creating a unique outcome.

Working within visual communication is a lot like this; each new piece of work leads on from the last, an approach is adopted. Within that approach should be room for experimentation and new invention. The more you perfect your craft, the more you realize there is to learn.

ANTHONY BURRILL

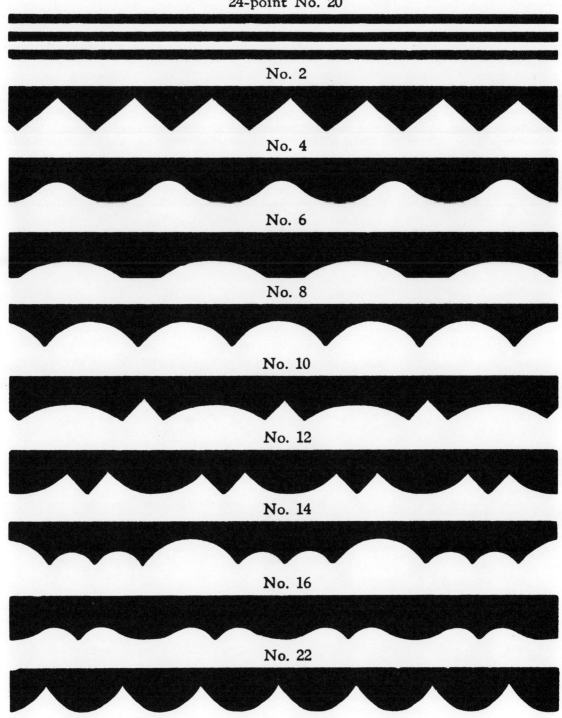

24-point No. 20

No. 2

No. 4

No. 6

No. 8

No. 10

No. 12

No. 14

No. 16

No. 22

AAAAAAAAAAAAAA
AAAABBBBCI
CCCCCCCDI
DDDDDDDDE
EEEEEEEEEE
EEEEEEEEEFFF

Peel-off letterforms arranged in a repeat pattern that makes economical use of manufacturing and materials. Fitting in each letter as tightly as possible to its neighbours, and filling all available space. Cramming in the letters to make an abstract study in geometric forms; a concrete tone poem of pure aesthetic.

This jaunty letter R is from a letterpress type sample book, itself a rich storehouse of typographic invention. This letterform looks contemporary but was originally drawn in the early part of the last century. It still seems fresh; its youthful good looks have not been diminished by time.

As a designer it's crucial to look at as much typographic reference as possible, and to understand the history of typography. Not just from books and digital sources, but by looking at the world around. Fragments of type can be spotted everywhere on the street. Forgotten road signs, faded shop fronts and crumbling advertisements are easy to miss, but by looking in hidden-away places you can still see traces of the former streetscape.

You might be surprised at how contemporary some of this historical material looks. We have a blinkered view of the past, but by searching for quirky examples a different view of it can be found.

ANTHONY BURRILL

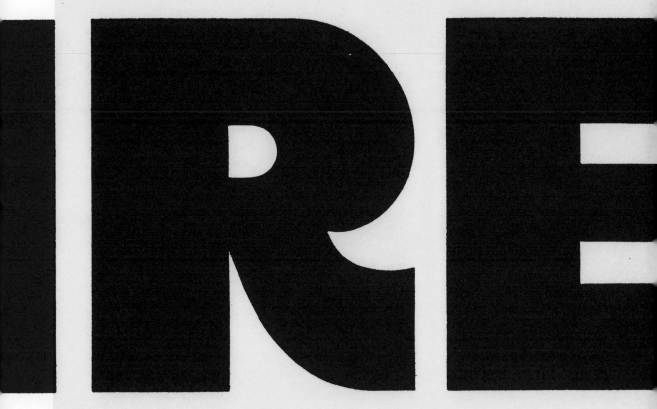

16-line No. 281

12-line No. 282

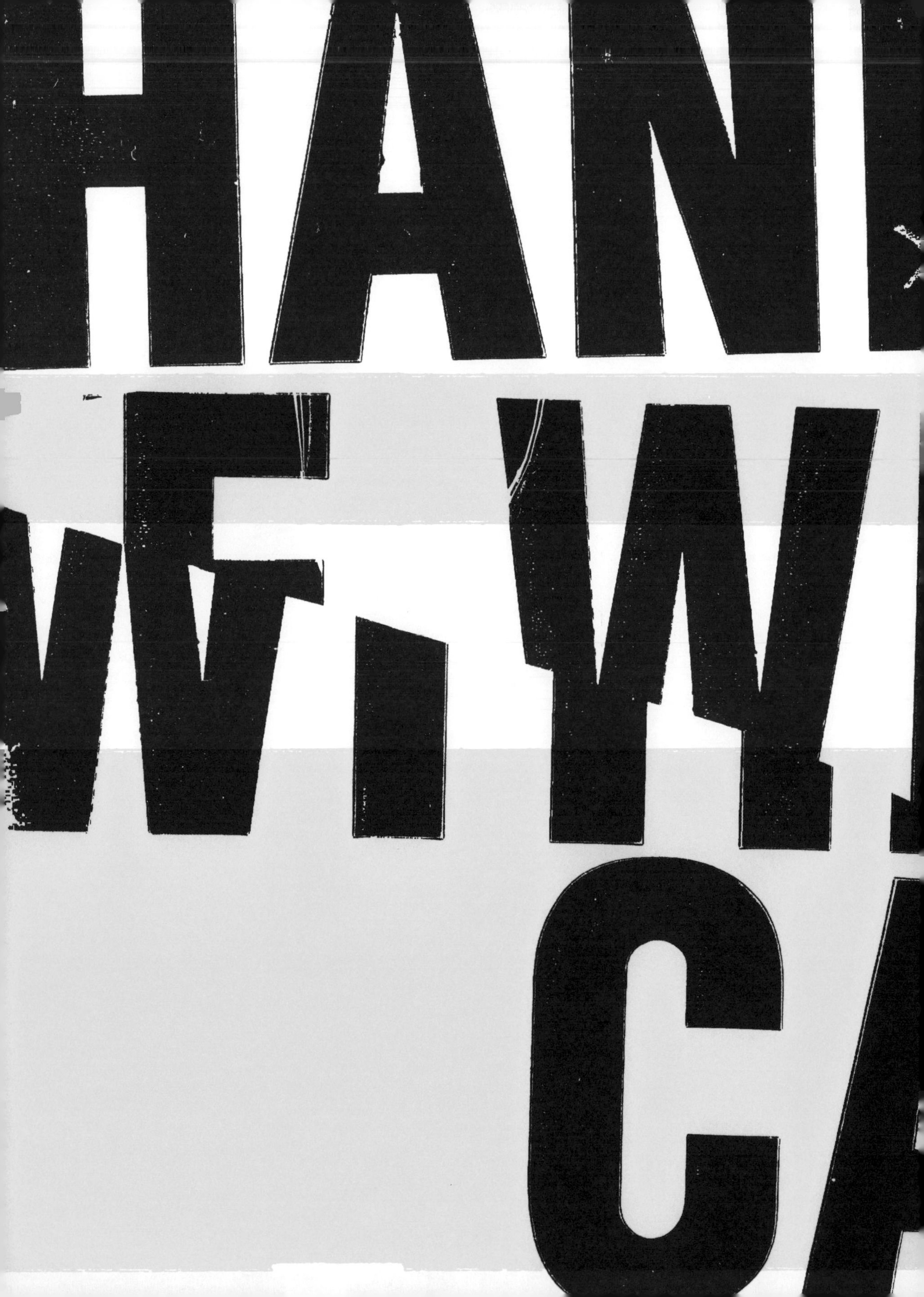

This wall is a collage of older building materials that have been salvaged and repurposed. The jumble of images and symbols has the feel of a scrapbook, constructed out of stone rather than paper.

Slowly peeling vinyl reveals new expressive letterforms created by the effects of failing adhesive. The curling of the material adds an organic character to this standard typeface.

ANTHONY BURRILL

An isolated letter A sits happily in the centre of a generous circle, from A to B and back again.

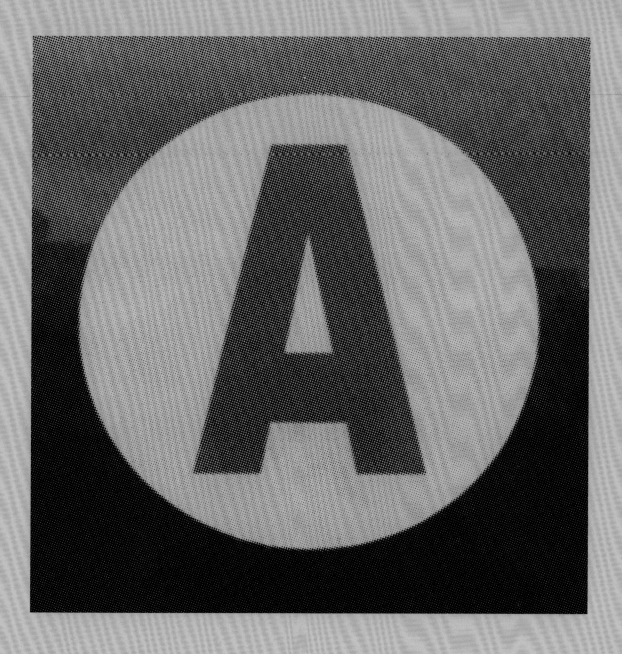

LOOK & SEE

Hand-carved geometric letterforms have a powerful incised beauty, their visual form dictated by their physicality. I like to focus in on letters, examining their construction and signs of human touch. I like how the restrictions of process and materials affect the finished design.

ANTHONY BURRILL

This way and that way, go here or go there, you'll end up in the same place.

LOOK & SEE

Simple geometric roundels divided in half have a satisfying visual simplicity. They warn us off, bar us from entry, restrict our movement. How this message has come to be represented in this form is fascinating; we all understand what it means, yet it is abstract and makes no reference to the physical space we are in.

ANTHONY BURRILL

A smashed sign clinging to its original form, still letting us know what number it is, just about.

LOOK & SEE

Car number plates are everywhere, but are subtly different in each country you visit. These examples are extremely geometric, designed with a quirky flair.

ANTHONY BURRILL

The three is the star, grabbing the limelight with its curious unbalanced character.

Slowly disintegrating fire door signs, showing the effects of time and wear. We can still just about make out what they say.

ANTHONY BURRILL

it helps that they are in a series, with each iteration filling in the blanks of its neighbour.

Looking closely at a sign on a wall in Italy. The unusual character of these condensed letterforms is low-slung and high-waisted at the same time; quite a feat. These quirks of type design are everywhere and easy to miss. Focus in tightly on found graphics in the street, and see something new every day.

236 ANTHONY BURRILL

A crude dot-matrix rendering of a three-letter word that at first appears as an abstract design. Using repetition in both letterform and layout, this industrial example looks like a poem, the substance of the words evaporating in the fresh air.

Spotted in Bangkok, this Thai stencil is a beautiful variation on a theme, each character embellished with a variety of elements.

ANTHONY BURRILL

There is something oddly appealing about this vertically stacked **PIZZA**. The haphazard, awkward arrangement of letters feels wrong, almost as if the tower is about to topple or is in the process of falling over.

LOOK & SEE

A railway logo transposed into reflective signage that still looks strong and geometric. The sense of speed and direction is communicated in a few bold shapes.

ANTHONY BURRILL

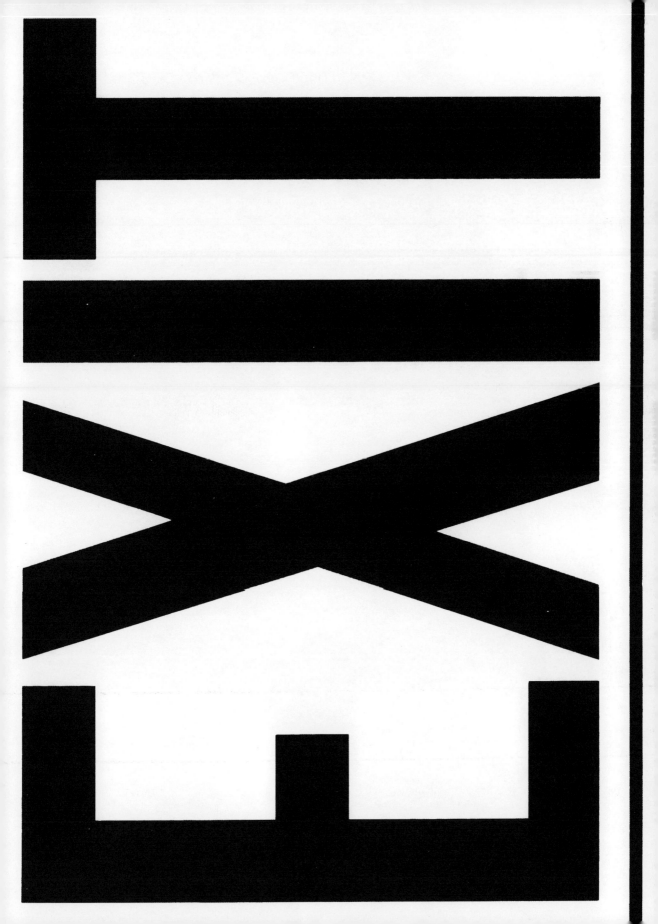

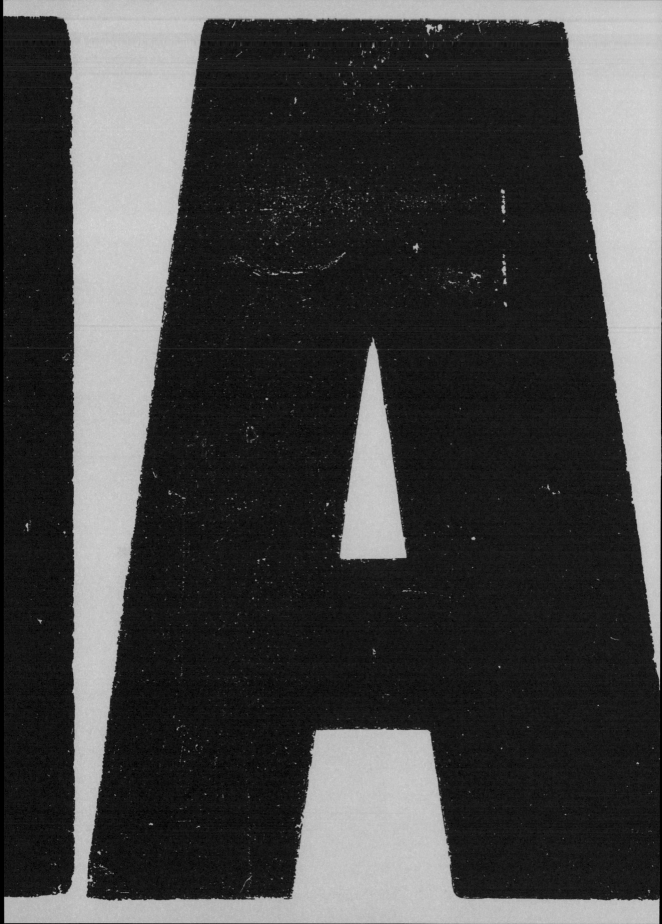

There is an anarchic joy to be had in seeing odd combinations of typefaces that shouldn't work together but somehow do.

It's a tantalising glimpse behind the scenes in the land that taste forgot, suggesting an alternative universe of design that flouts conventional wisdom.

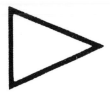

We normally think of stencil typefaces as simple geometric letterforms, designed for function rather than decoration. But this example from Mexico doesn't follow these rules.

These crazy letterforms wouldn't work so well marking an emergency exit. You would be far too occupied admiring their rounded forms to make a quick escape. So the results of using this stencil could potentially be fatal. Use with caution!

If nothing else, this stencil proves that it's possible to make any typeface into a stencil. Whether you should do this is another question.

I think in this case it was worth flouting the strict laws of stencil design to produce this once-in-a-lifetime display font.

ANTHONY BURRILL

ABCD

HOPQ

Zabel

ABCDEFGHI
JKLMNOPQR
STUVWXYZ
12345
67890

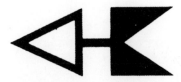

A type sample of a wood letter font was commissioned by my friend Tim while he was living and working in Jamaica. Tim and I studied graphic design at the Royal College of Art, and soon after we graduated he took up a teaching job in Kingston, Jamaica.

There he discovered a print shop that produced flyers for local party nights using a combination of letterpress and screen print. Tim commissioned a series of posters from the printer and posted them back to friends in London.

Every few months we'd receive an update in the form of a visual diary; a list of dates and events rendered in beautiful letterpress. Together these mini posters gave his friends back in England an insight into his daily life.

Hands up who still owns a fax machine.
No, me neither.

My first encounter with the new and
exciting world of data transmission
was at art college in the 1990s. The fax
machine in the graphics office was a
thing of wonder and a source of great
interest. How could a drawing be fed in
and digitally pulverized, then magically
transmitted over time and space by this
anonymous-looking grey box?

We were all in thrall to this new piece
of kit. The graphic language of the fax
spawned a new visual aesthetic that
influenced the early adopters of digital
technology. However, I was wary of this
rival to my beloved photocopier. The
fax lacked the warm aesthetic of the
machine that had shaped my graphic
development.

A few times I tried enlarging bitmapped
type from the fax on the photocopier.
But it was an unhappy marriage. I
found it hard to love the mechanical
halftones and jagged type effects of
the interloper.

I needn't have worried, though. The
reign of the fax machine as a creative
tool was to be short-lived; it was
superseded within a few years by
scanners and desktop computers.

 **DOCUMENT TO BE FAXED**

 **DOCUMENT TO BE FAXED**

 **DOCUMENT TO BE FAXED**

 **DOCUMENT TO BE FAXED**

 **DOCUMENT TO BE FAXED**

 **DOCUMENT TO BE FAXED**

75mm ● ○

This is a lovely upper-case E from the Letraset catalogue I've had since I began studying graphic design back in the 1980s. I particularly like the nicely extended proportions of this letter. It's a cool E. Geometric in design and free of any ornamentation, it looks classical in form, almost sculptural. Hard-edged and modern; a purely rational, forward-facing character.

Next time you receive a utility bill or an official-looking letter, have a look at the envelope itself. It's the first thing I do; rather than looking at how much the bill is, I'm distracted by the striking repeat pattern printed inside the envelope.

The pattern isn't just there for decoration; it is designed to disrupt the text inside, making it difficult to decipher confidential information.

The pattern reminds me of military camouflage designs, with their role being to disguise, hide and disrupt. When examined closely they are revealed as op-art inspired fields of pure eye-boggling repetition.

I'm intrigued by this area of design. It is purely functional but produces beautiful artwork as an unintentional side-effect.

ANTHONY BURRILL

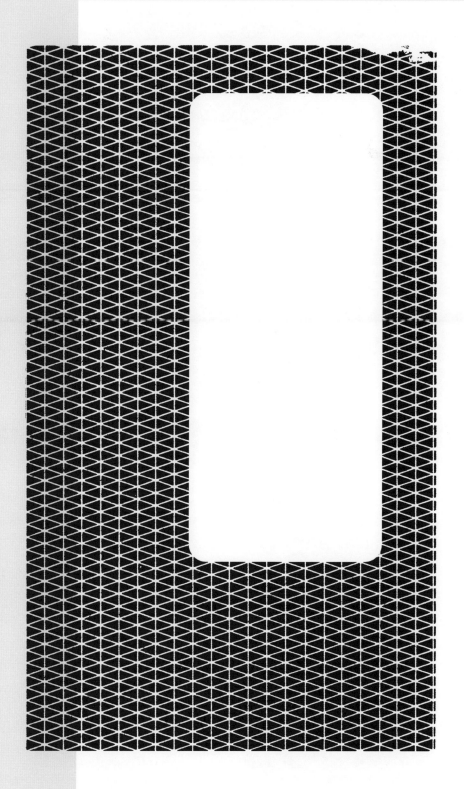

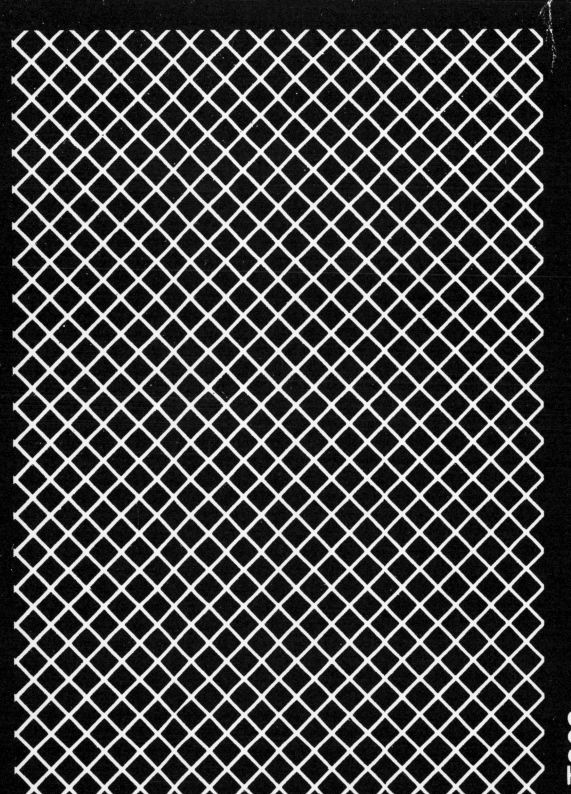

LT928

FRAGILE
FRAGILE
FRAGILE
FRAGILE

FRAGILE
FRAGILE
FRAGILE
FRAGILE

FRAGILE
FRAGILE
FRAGILE
FRAGILE

FRAGILE
FRAGILE
FRAGILE
FRAGILE

FRAGILE
FRAGILE
FRAGILE
FRAGILE

FRAGILE
FRAGILE
FRAGILE
FRAGILE

FRAGILE
FRAGILE
FRAGILE
FRAGILE

FRAGILE
FRAGILE
FRAGILE
FRAGILE

ILE
ILE
ILE
ILE

ILE
ILE
ILE
ILE

To say that these letterforms are quite condensed is like saying that Mount Everest is quite high. These letters are ridiculously condensed, the tallest and thinnest letters I've ever seen. The amazing thing is that they are still legible; even with this extreme amount of distortion it is possible to make out the words without much effort.

Even more incredible is that these letters are found in a wood type specimen book. These fragile-looking letters were commercially available, manufactured out of wood. It's hard to imagine the precision required to make these letters with such exacting tolerances.

The primary use for these elongated oddities would have been on theatre and music hall posters, where many performers' names were squeezed into a small amount of space. It was as a result of these requirements that the letters became so ridiculously distorted, almost to the point of illegibility. This is where typography becomes abstracted by the constraints of the medium.

ANTHONY BURRILL

ELONGATED SANS No. 323

40-line   16-line   ELON

40-line

GR SCARBORO

GR

20-line

GR ORCHEST

GR

SEE THIS PUNCH MARK   DELITTLE YORK   *STAM*

THE STRAND

VALID UNTIL

WE 09

14:43

ENTRY TIME

These brittle numbers and letters are the product of the most minimal print technology, and have a tough beauty. The letterforms are reduced to a raw grid of jagged steps that feel sculptural.

The sparse detail has been reduced in order to save on information and data. Everything superfluous has been taken away from these characters and reduced to the edge of legibility.

Within this brutal aesthetic there is much to admire. The apparent crudity of the letterforms has been has been reduced to the essence of understanding, challenging notions of readability and beauty along the way.

A family of graphic arrows are made up
of interchangeable elements to create
a number of variations. Designed for the
constraints of letterpress, this flexible
system enables the designer to use a
variety of arrow sizes.

I love graphic systems and how they
can be expanded on; even the simplest
system can suggest a whole graphic
language. From this example I can
imagine an entire family of letterforms
based on a small number of geometric
elements combined.

The idea of a kit of parts or a modular
system lies at the heart of many graphic
systems. Everything is based on a
matrix that provides a link between
all elements.

Breaking graphic design down to
this molecular level allows us to build
complex systems from a small number
of parts, making multiple potential
outcomes.

Being able to judge these outcomes and
selecting the most successful is the role
of the designer, and this is informed by
taste and fashion as much as technical
knowledge. How a design makes you
feel is as important as what it is saying.
Visual communication connects with
both your intellect and your emotions.

ANTHONY BURRILL

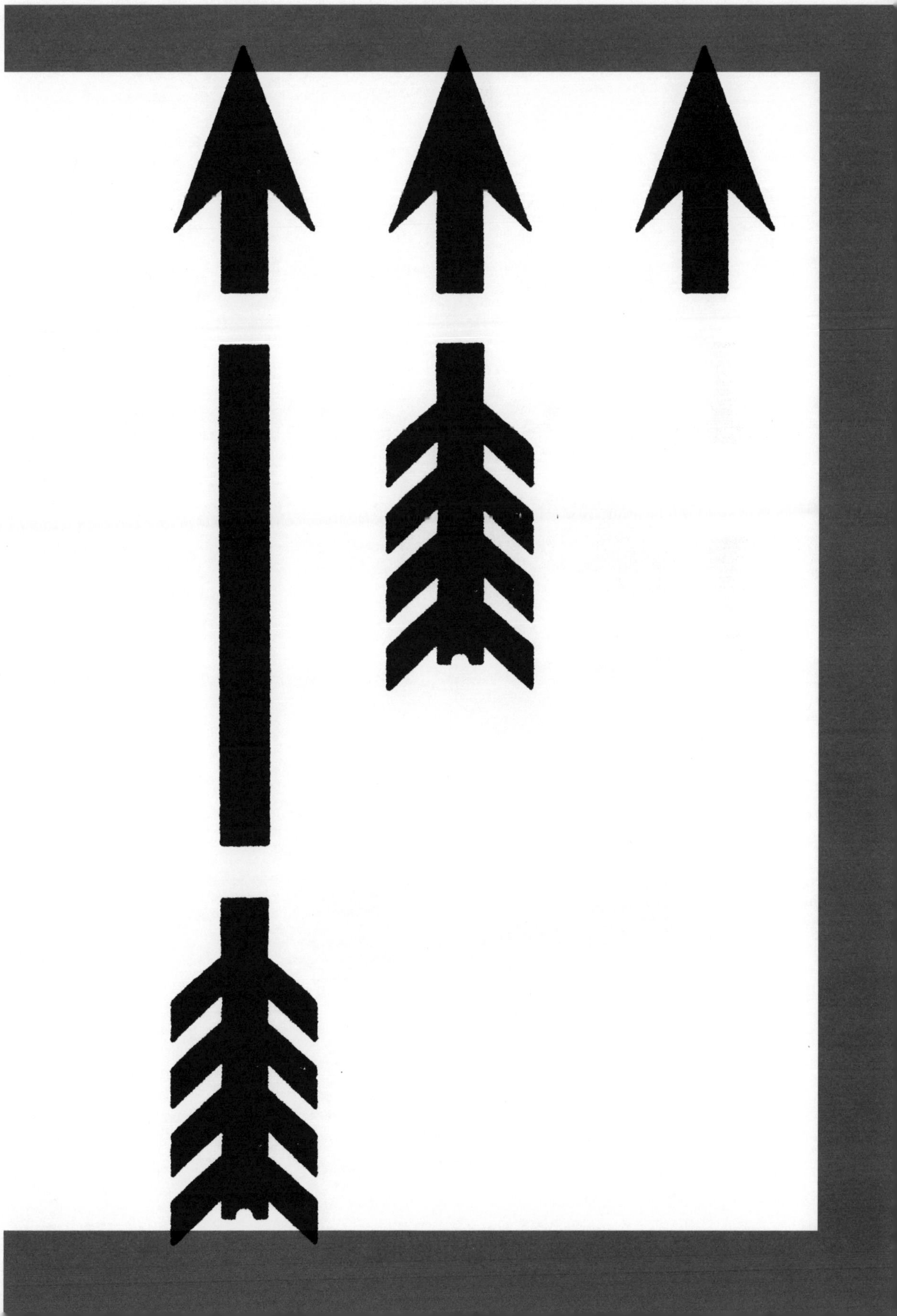

MARDI

27

NOVEMBRE

331-034   S SÉVERIN   48

☀ 7 h 19, 15 h 57   ☾ le 30, ⊕ le 7

365 days printed on to Bible paper, the flimsiest of materials. Every day is represented with the same simple layout: huge numerals, day and month, laid out with sparse beauty. Start the day by tearing off yesterday and discarding it. Today is a new start, full of promise and potential.

Do not drop!

This is the way up.

There is no up without down.

Up needs down and down needs up.

Which way is up?

ANTHONY BURRILL

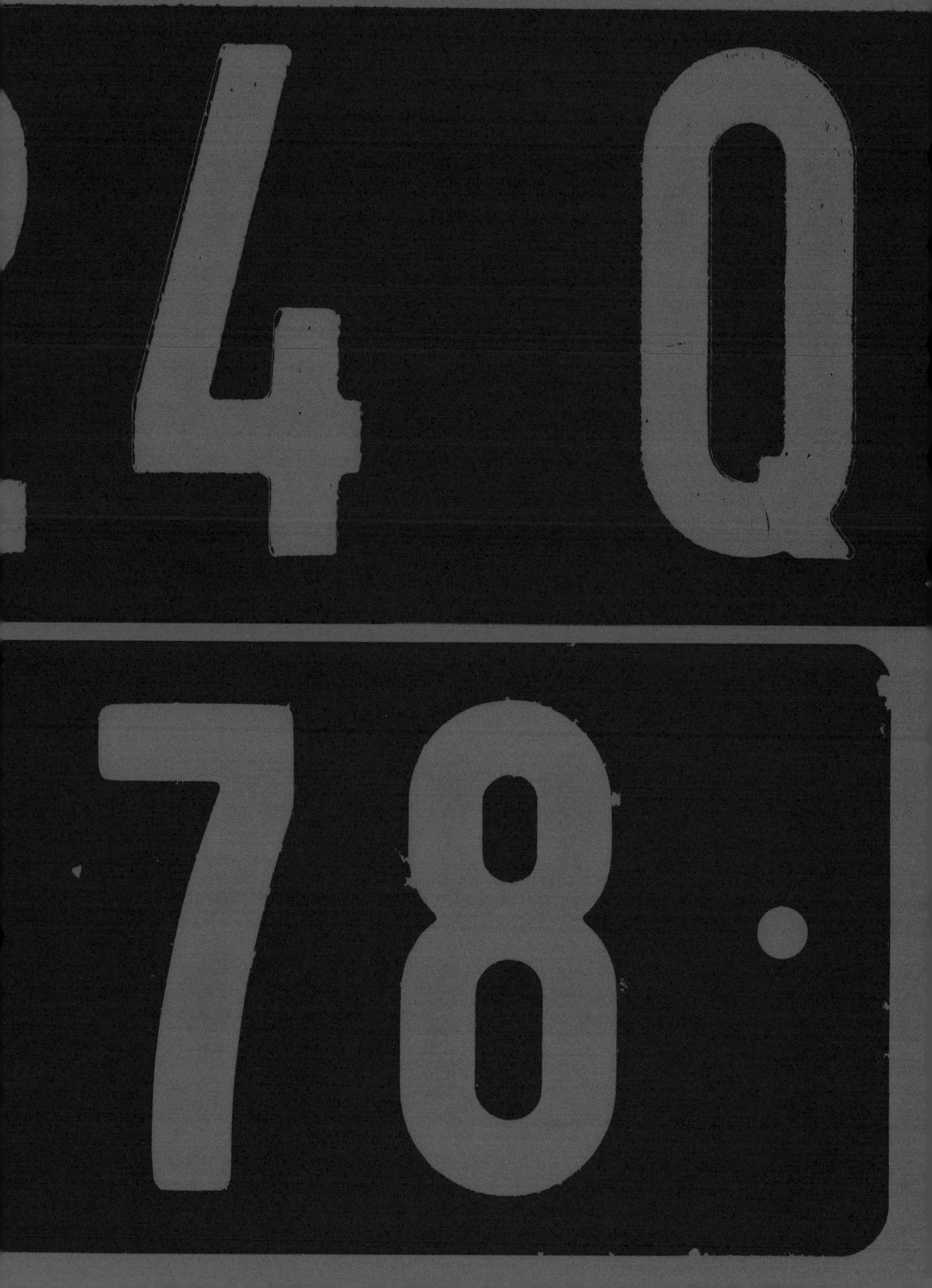
4Q
78

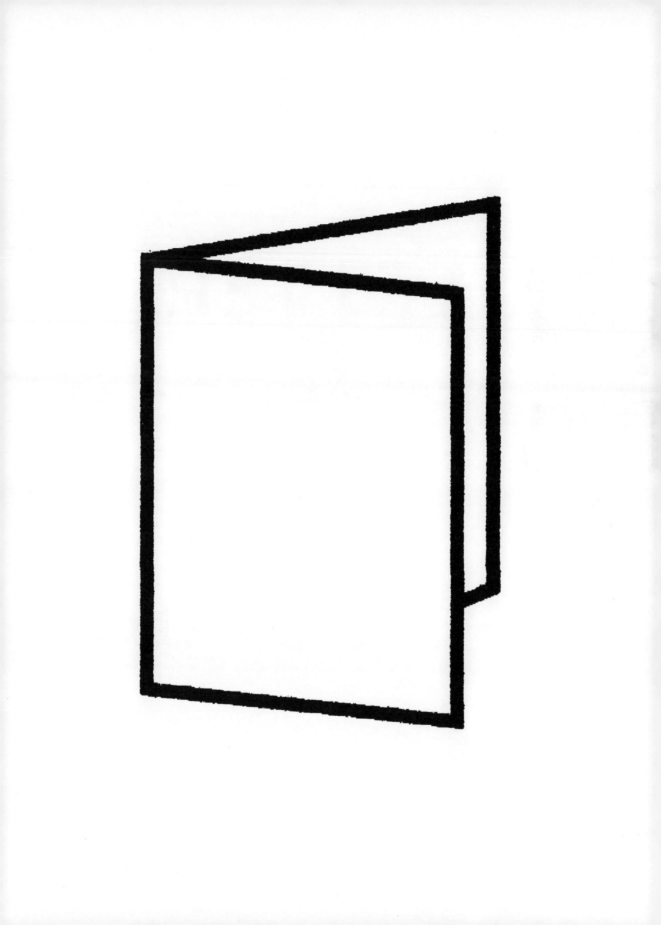

A satisfying vertical arrangement of
slab-like videotapes, drawn in a strange
perspective that enhances their already
robotic appearance.

Building blocks stand to attention
forming an impenetrable wall of data.
Chunks of information are monolithic in
a featureless expanse of space.

Information is stored securely within
these robust custodians of handicam
footage; an Easter Island figure time-
capsule for the future.

ANTHONY BURRILL

Store vertically
Rangez verticalement

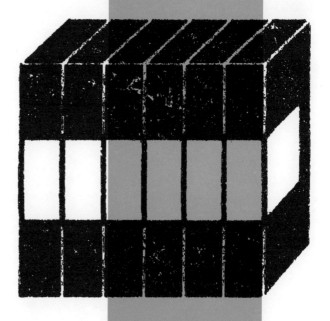

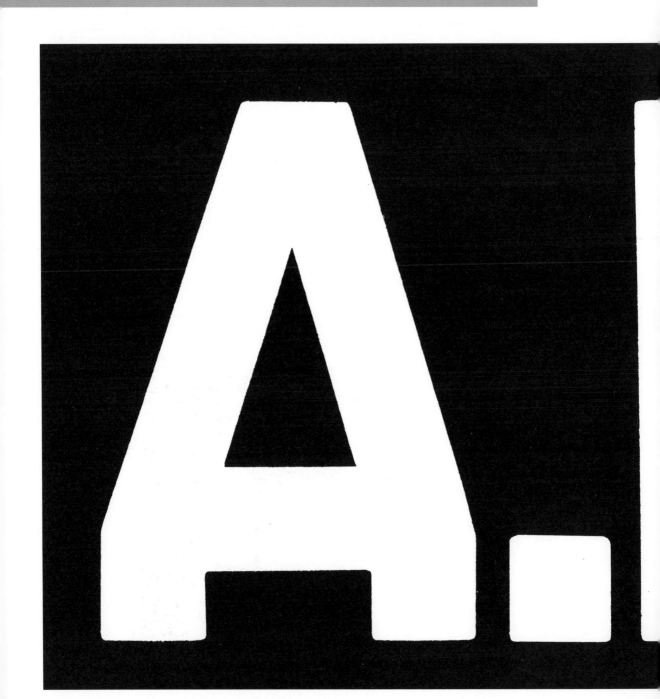

This letter A is stuck to the front cover of a notebook; the other letter that you can't see is B. I found these letters in my local hardware store, in an old stack at the back of a shelf. This is where the good stuff lurks, the long-forgotten remnants of out-of-stock items.

These letters were being sold off cheap, so I got them all. Not quite a complete alphabet, but enough to enjoy. The letterform is based on the standard car number plate typeface. Maybe these stick-on letters were intended to provide auxiliary identification for the trailers and caravans.

The awkward shape of the A is lovely. Its low centre of gravity and chunky base make it look friendly and approachable.

LOOK & SEE

This lively abstract design is found
inside a packet of coloured stickers,
hidden behind the product within
the cellophane wrapper. The design
cheerfully displays the full range of
stickers available, a collector's guide
to these colourful pieces of office
stationery.

Arranged this way they resemble
an abstract painting, with a feeling
of weightlessness and motion. A
momentary snapshot of geometric
forms in freefall.

ANTHONY BURRILL

The repeated message stacked high on a wine glass.

This goblet of fragility a reminder of shattered dreams.

The familiar rattle of broken contents on the doormat.

The clumsy delivery.

Please, handle with care.

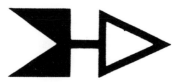

A range of dots and circles: large circles
close up, and small circles far away.
A chart used to display letterpress
borders in varying sizes and weights.
Repeat patterns used for decoration
and viable for mass production.
Describing a landscape, perspective
diminishing into space. Moving through
a landscape of simple forms in space.

ANTHONY BURRILL

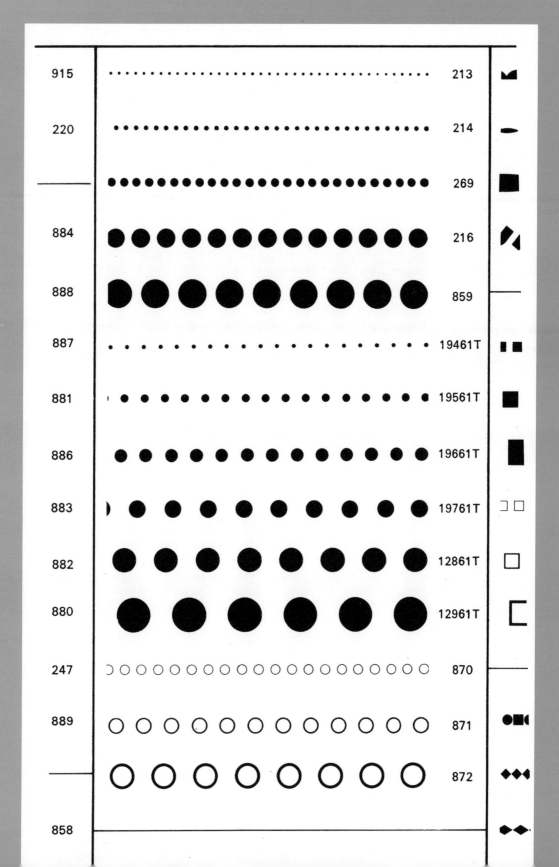

BENEFACTORS

Guillaume Adam
Vanesa Aguilera Hatero
Marcus Ainley
Alejandro Alcaraz
Karen Allain
Peter Allen
Kit Ambage
Silas Amos
Kei Aoki
Matthew Appleton
Alex Arias
Andy Arneil
Craig Atkinson
Nicola Bailey
Rebecca Ball
Jean-Charles Bassenne
Algy Batten
Lucy Bayley
David Bennett
Daniel Benneworth-Gray
Richard Berry
Mateusz Biel
Delphine Boardman
Ewoudt Boonstra
Otto Boreson
Jeremy Borgust
David Brimble
Eleanor Brittain
Matthew Brooks
Ewan Buck
Rachel Buntrock
Dan Catalin Burzo
Andrew Bybee
Catherine Byng
Brian Byrne
Michele Byrne
David Cabianca
Phill Capewell
Danie Carey
JR Chandler
Chung-Yang Chen
Jonathan Clay
Dave Clayton
Jonnie Clout
Ben Collier-Marsh
Steven Colvin-Whyte
Rhianne Connelly
Andy Cooke
Daniel Cookney
Paul Copeland
Christian Corless
Nicoleta Costin
Matt Coyne
Tom Crabtree
Eleanor Cross
Rachel Dalton
James Darcey
Rebecca Darcey
Morgan Davies
Tracey Day
Niek de Bruijn
Karel De Mulder
Fred Deakin
Kit Debuse

Donna DeForbes
Davy Denduyver
Caroline Denyer
Jane Shaw Dietrich
Alexandre Dimos
Tom Doidge
Fraser Donachie
Aine Donovan
Paul Downey
Ned Drew
Hope Drummond
Matt Eastwood
Jonathan Elliman
Liz Elliott
Elena Etter
Lewie Evans
Steve Fachiri
Jason Fagg
Ean Faragher
Brent Fernandez
Mark Foster
Rich French
Cathy Gale
Kieran Gardner
Rachel Garry
Tim George
Bobby Gillespie
Alexandra Grace Wylde Glinn
Geir Goosen
Stuart Graham
Jaume Grau
Nick Green
Andrew Greenhouse
Ellie Grout
Anna Grupka
Hugo Gstrein
Neil Gurr
David Hadley
Carl Halford
Martin Hamilton
Ben Hamman
Tim Harbour
Simon Harris
Elliot Hartwell
Harvey Lloyd Screens
Anders Hellstrand
Michael Henein
Cole Henley
Jessica Herbert
Borja Hernández
Marc-Antoine Herrmann
Matt Higgins
James Hill
Meredith Hill
Matt Hilton
Mark Hirons
Sally Hope
Martin Hopkins
Lindsay Howarth
James Howley
Greg Hughes
Keith Humphrey
Philip Hunt
Stephen Hynes
Mark Hyson

Mikkel Inumineq
Chris Ireland
JackGDesign
Brandon Jameson
Jimbo
Aaron Johnson
Hojab Jomehri
Elen Jones
Babs Jossi
Edward Jung
Lauren Jury Armitage
Constance Kaine
Gareth Kay
Robert Kelemen
Jake Kenny
Merryn Kerrigan
Marcel Khan
Maria Khoshaba
Lottie Kingdon
Leo Kipen
Jesse Kirsch
Steve Kroeter
Jennifer Lamping
Andrew Langhorn
Ollie Langridge
Jose Luis Lanzagorta
David Laranjeira
Kelly Lawlor
Jonathan Lawrence
Haiminh Le
Sean Leahy
Luis Leal Pereira
George Lee
Eric Leon
James Letherby
David Livingston
Mike Lomas
Kevin Long
Quique López
Ruben Lourens
Joe Lovelock
Mark Lundberg
Kim Lundgren
Mark Magowan
Ben Malbon
Katie Marcus
Diego Marini
Craig May
Kathleen McConaughy
Thomas McInally
Luke McLaughlin
Joy McMillan
James Mellor
Teodorik Menšl
Stephen Mildwater
Steve Milne
Christine Miocque
Mimeartist Limited
Kat Molesworth
John Montgomery
Annalisa Morgan
Sarah Morris
Ben Mottershead
Chris Mount
Poul Mundbjerg

Paul Neale
Henry Neves-Charge
Dean Newcombe
Jack Newman
Daniel Nieuwenhuizen
Chris Norman
Silvia Novak
Anthony Oram
Christopher Orozco
Tom Otteson
John Owens
Neil Palfreyman
Simon Palmer
Marina Pape
John Parker
Alex Pataca
Hinal Patel
Cody Paulson
Paulpod
David Payne
John Peck
Beth Peek
Matteo Pelo
Ginny Pickles
Yee Poon
Russell Potter
Martin Power
Boakye Prempeh
Michael Preston
Kirian Procyk
Jamie Prokell
Martin Pyper at Me Studio
Luna Raphael
Simon Ray
Piero Regnante
Scott Rench
Nigel Reyes
Sean Reynolds
Daniel Richardson
Craig Riseborough
Liam Roberts
Tom Roebuck
Paul Rogers
Donna Romano
Marc Rouleau
Timothy Rowe
Jacek Rudzki
Tim Salter
Martin Sanne Kristiansen
Rob Saunders
Henry Saunderson
Chelsea Schilling
Carl Seal
Miles Shirley
Benjamin K Shown
Cas Simons
Nikki Sims
Chet Slater Design
Christopher Slevin
Andrew Smith
Richard Spellman
Daniela Spinelli
Katie Stapleton
Michael Stearns

Sandro Stefanelli
Roo Stenning
James Stiff
Paul Stimpson
Scott Stowell
Jason Sturgill
Mike Tamis
Kam Tang
Rupert Thornborough
Will Timney
Joshua To
Sara To
Christian Tönsmann
Domenico Torti
Regis Tosetti
Kenny Tran
Sean Tucker
UPPERCASE magazine
Matt Uminski
Carlos Valencia
Kyle van Blerk
Claire Vickers
Albert Virgili
Alex Vissaridis
Tomi Vollauschek
Mathew Voyce
Killian Walsh
Gregor Watson
Ren Watson
Mary Waygood
Oliver Webley
Namalee Weerasekara
Rebecca Westwood
Steve Whapshott
Caspian Whistler
Reuben Whitehouse
Jason R Whiting
Debbie Wigglesworth
Jonathan Wilkinson
Emma Williams
Ray Wong
Caroline Wooden
Charles Worrall
Jie-Fei Yang
Remi Zed
Karen Zimmermann

Anthony Burrill would like to thank:
Darren Wall, Lucas Dietrich, Emma Burrill,
Tim Lewis, Nigel Robinson, Paul Neale,
Patrick Thomas, Erik Kessels, Anthony Peters,
Paul Plowman and Jeremy Tankard.

First published in the United Kingdom in 2018
by Thames & Hudson Ltd, 181A High Holborn,
London WC1V 7QX

This book was produced by Volume: vol.co

British Library Cataloguing-in-Publication Data
A catalogue record for this book is available
from the British Library

ISBN 978-0-500-02211-5

Printed and bound in China by C & C Offset Printing
Co. Ltd.

To find out about all our publications, please visit
www.thamesandhudson.com. There you can subscribe
to our e-newsletter, browse or download our current
catalogue, and buy any titles that are in print.

3898·PT 78

KLMNOPRS 3

3898·PT 78